ITIL® 4 Essentials

Your essential guide for the ITIL 4 Foundation
exam and beyond

Second edition

ITIL® 4 Essentials

Your essential guide for the ITIL 4 Foundation exam and beyond

Second edition

CLAIRE AGUTTER

IT Governance Publishing

IT Governance Publishing Ltd
Unit 3, Clive Court
Bartholomew's Walk
Cambridgeshire Business Park
Ely, Cambridgeshire
CB7 4EA
United Kingdom
www.itgovernancepublishing.co.uk

Formerly published as *ITIL® Lifecycle Essentials – Your essential guide for the ITIL Foundation exam and beyond* in 2013 by IT Governance Publishing.

First published in the United Kingdom in 2019 by IT Governance Publishing

ISBN 978-1-78778-158-0

Second edition published in the United Kingdom in 2020 by IT Governance Publishing

ISBN 978-1-78778-218-1

FOREWORD

Congratulations! You are now in possession of a book that will prove to be of great value to IT professionals at different stages in their IT service management journey: from the ITIL® greenhorns to the veterans looking to solidify their status.

ITIL 4 Essentials has been written with a delightfully refreshing approach, one that combines theoretical knowledge with practical know-how, arising from the author's real-world experience. The author has also painstakingly marked out sections that are specific to the ITIL 4 Foundation certification exam as an easy reference for those who intend to attempt it.

Large volumes of theory can often be exhausting and at times uninteresting. One of the standout features in *ITIL 4 Essentials* is how the author overcomes this by encouraging active participation from the reader through the 'Have a go' exercises wherever appropriate. The 'Practice considerations' that have been documented add tremendous value to anyone looking to implement various aspects of ITIL 4, as the author shares her real-world concerns and constraints.

For those new to ITIL 4, the Service Value System has been covered extensively, with particular emphasis on 'The 7 guiding principles' and the '34 ITIL practices'.

This book is a must-have item on your desk for its simplicity in presentation, thoroughness in detail and pragmatism in approach.

Sanjay Nair

PREFACE

I've been involved with ITIL® and IT service management for more than 15 years. In that time, I've worked in operational and consulting roles, before setting up my own training and consulting organisations. I know from my professional and personal experience how satisfying it is when technology works, and how frustrating it can be when it doesn't.

When writing this book, I noticed that, while there are many ITSM publications available, there is still little practical guidance for the new ITSM practitioner. There is a wide range of 'exam pass' guides, but these don't add much value once your exam is complete.

This book contains everything you need to know to pass the ITIL 4 Foundation Certificate, but much more as well.

I've covered practices and concepts that are not addressed as part of the Foundation syllabus, and provided practical tips for applying service management. I've added to the theory by including practice considerations, based on my experiences.

As you proceed through the book, you can easily see which content is related to the ITIL 4 Foundation syllabus, and which isn't.

Content related to the Foundation syllabus is highlighted with this symbol:

Content that is not part of the Foundation syllabus is highlighted with this symbol:

Unless stated otherwise, all quotations are from *ITIL®Foundation, ITIL 4 edition.*

I wish you every success in your ITIL Foundation exam and hope you will continue to use this book as you work with IT service management in your day-to-day role.

Claire Agutter
Director
ITSM Zone/Scopism

ABOUT THE AUTHOR

Claire Agutter is a service management trainer, consultant and author. In 2017 and 2018 she was recognised as an HDI Top 25 Thought Leader in Technical Support and Service Management and was part of the team that won itSMF UK's 2017 Thought Leadership Award. Claire is the host of the popular ITSM Crowd hangouts and Chief Architect for VeriSM. She is the director of ITSM Zone, which provides online IT service management training, and Scopism, a content and consulting organisation.

After providing training to thousands of successful Foundation candidates, Claire has written this book to provide essential guidance for ITSM practitioners preparing for their ITIL® 4 Foundation exam. The book also provides practical guidance on the application of ITIL and ITSM concepts in their workplace.

For more information, please see:

- *https://itsm.zone*;
- *www.scopism.com*; and
- Contact: *www.linkedin.com/in/claireagutter/*.

ACKNOWLEDGEMENTS

I would like to thank Anna Leyland; managing consultant at Sopra Steria UK Limited and Sanjay Nair; helpdesk manager at his current workplace, for their time and helpful comments during the development of this book.

CONTENTS

Contents

Contents

Contents

Contents

CHAPTER 1: KEY CONCEPTS OF SERVICE MANAGEMENT

We're going to start by taking a look at what service management actually means. Service management describes a way of working within an organisation that helps to deliver value to the organisation's customers, so it is worth spending time analysing its definition, along with some of the related concepts.

Why is service management important?

In today's world, information technology (IT) is a fully integrated part of everyone's life. Whether using a smartphone, withdrawing cash from an ATM, paying bills, or booking tickets on the Internet, IT is present in everything we do. It often plays a supporting role, so we don't even think about what we are using until it stops working.

In the modern business organisation, we see the same reliance on IT and IT-enabled services. Every department, from finance and customer services through to logistics, relies on IT to carry out its role effectively and efficiently. Effectiveness refers to whether IT is able to achieve its objectives. Efficiency refers to whether IT uses an appropriate amount of resources. An efficient IT organisation will use optimal amounts of time, money, staff, etc.

Now, more than ever, organisations need effective and efficient IT to survive. IT supports critical business processes that generate revenue, serve customers and allow business goals to be achieved. At the same time, the IT department or

IT organisation is under more and more pressure to deliver better services, often at a reduced cost. It needs to find a balance between supply and demand, service cost and service quality.

To make sure that IT can support business objectives properly, organisations need service management. Service management makes sure that the IT-enabled services delivered do what the business needs, when the business needs it.

With effective support and good-quality IT-enabled services, organisations can adopt bold strategies, including the expansion of existing services and movement into new markets. With poor-quality services, organisations will struggle to deliver what they do now, let alone expand and offer anything new or exciting. Now, when many organisations are adopting a strategy focused on 'digital transformation', this topic becomes even more relevant.

Why use ITIL® for service management?

It is worthwhile asking 'what is ITIL and why is it important?' ITIL is considered best practice for IT service management (ITSM). It was originally developed by the UK government, and is now adopted by many organisations in both the public and private sectors globally.

ITIL is not a prescriptive standard that must be followed. It does not say what must be done in a service provider organisation, and there is no certificate or award for successfully adopting ITIL in an organisation. Instead, ITIL is a framework that organisations can adopt and adapt to improve the way they deliver their IT-enabled services.

ITIL is a widely recognised source of best practice. It supports organisations as they deliver services that meet their customers' needs, at a price the customer is willing to pay.

In today's economic climate, organisations cannot afford to stand still. They need to review their performance and compare it to their competitors and make sure they are improving constantly. Using best practice available in the public domain can support internal improvement.

This thinking doesn't just apply to the private sector. Public-sector organisations, such as local and central government departments, also need to demonstrate that they offer quality services and value for money. They might not be measured on profit, but there will be service objectives that they have to meet.

A brief history of ITIL

ITIL was developed by the UK government in the 1980s to help improve the quality of IT-enabled services and IT projects. The Central Computer and Telecommunications Agency (CCTA, later renamed the Office of Government Commerce) was tasked with developing a framework for efficient and financially responsible use of IT resources in a government environment.

The earliest version of ITIL was called the Government Information Technology Infrastructure Management (GITIM). GITIM focused on service support and service delivery, but was very different from the current version of ITIL. Large companies and government agencies started to adopt ITIL, spreading service management practices across the globe.

In 2000, Microsoft® used ITIL to develop the Microsoft Operations Framework. In 2001, version 2 of ITIL was released, with training based on the Service Support and Service Delivery core publications. Hundreds of thousands of people around the world took ITIL training and achieved certification to help them manage IT-enabled services and environments, and progress in their ITSM careers.

In 2007, version 3 of ITIL was released, with an update to v3 in 2011. ITIL v3 was based around a service lifecycle that included:

- Service strategy
- Service design
- Service transition
- Service operation
- Continual service improvement

The newest ITIL version is ITIL 4. Released in 2019, ITIL 4 has evolved to a value system-focused approach that can be integrated with other management practices and ways of working, such as Agile and DevOps.

Why has ITIL been successful?

ITIL is not academic and theoretical. It is based on the experience of ITSM practitioners and offers a practical approach that has evolved over many years. The introduction of a value system-focus in ITIL 4 means that organisations must concentrate less on technology and more on how to co-create value with either internal or external customers. Common processes and practices and a strong service management framework all help to support the focus on value.

ITIL is successful because it is:

- **Vendor neutral:** ITIL is not linked to one supplier, or one technology, or one industry. This means it can be adopted across all types and sizes of organisation.
- **Non-prescriptive:** Organisations need to adopt and adapt the elements of ITIL that work for them and their customers.
- **Best practice:** ITIL draws on experience from service management practitioners across the globe.

Best practice simply means:

Proven activities or processes that have been successfully used in multiple organizations.[1]

ITIL is seen as being preferable to the proprietary knowledge that builds up inside organisations and the minds of staff members. Proprietary knowledge isn't usually documented in a consistent way. It exists because it has built up over time. This means it is not challenged or improved – and can create a real risk if an experienced staff member leaves and takes their proprietary knowledge with them.

In this chapter, we're going to take a look at some of the key concepts related to service management.

---

[1]

https://en.wikiversity.org/wiki/IT_Service_Management/Service_Manag ement.

Remember to look out for the symbols that denote content related to the ITIL 4 Foundation syllabus. We'll be examining syllabus-related content in this chapter.

📋 Denotes syllabus-related content.

📋 Value

Products and services need to add value to consumers to be successful. Value is *"the perceived benefits, usefulness and importance of something"*.

Some products and services are directly purchased by consumers, such as bank accounts and mobile phones. If a consumer doesn't feel they are receiving value, the service provider organisation will know very quickly because the consumer will choose a different product or service, probably from a rival organisation.

Where the service relationship is defined less clearly, the service provider organisation might have to work harder to find out if their consumers feel that they are receiving value. For example, the television package that you pay for might include a news channel that you don't watch because you feel it's biased, so you consume news via the Internet instead. Because you still purchase the package, it's more difficult for your service provider to measure this and identify an improvement opportunity.

Value encompasses more than just 'value for money'. Some products and services are more expensive than others, but consumers choose them because they save time or convey status. Service provider organisations need to understand what it is that consumers value about their products and services. Services also need to create value for the service provider, to allow them to continue to provide the service in the future.

🗒 Service management

Services deliver **value** to consumers. If a service isn't carefully managed, the value might be less or might not be delivered at all. An IT-enabled service needs to be measured, monitored and maintained to continue working effectively. An IT organisation can't just put a service into the live environment and forget about it.

ITIL provides good practices for managing IT-enabled services. It doesn't matter what job you have in IT; your role is part of the overall service that is being offered to the consumer.

Most modern organisations rely on IT to be effective. They expect IT to be available and responsive, and communicate with them regularly. Technology alone does not deliver a good service. Technology needs to be managed to meet the customer's needs. The need for a more holistic approach to IT-enabled services is reflected in the four dimensions of service management described in the ITIL 4 guidance.

The definition of service management is:

"A set of specialized organizational capabilities for enabling value for customers in the form of services".

Capabilities refer to the ability of an organisation to carry out a task or activity. The more mature the organisation, the better its capabilities should be. Capabilities will be based on an organisation's experience of customers, processes, services, tools, market conditions, etc. This experience grows over time. Where an organisation has low or immature capabilities, it may choose to source capabilities from an external organisation.

An organisation can only develop these specialised organisational capabilities when it understands:

- The nature of value;
- The nature and scope of the stakeholders involved; and
- How value creation is enabled through services.

🌐 Service management as a professional practice

Service management should be viewed as a professional practice. It is supported by an extensive body of knowledge, experience and skills that has built up as the IT industry matured and developed a service focus.

There is a global community of professionals that supports service management, including organisations like the IT Service Management Forum. You can read more about the itSMF at *www.itsmfi.org*, including learning about your national chapter and any resources that are available to support you. The itSMF allows service management practitioners to connect with each other and share feedback, ideas and experiences.

The ITIL service management framework is supported by a scheme that provides quality assured education, training and certification. There are also other related training and certification schemes, covering areas such as project management, change management, business analysis, and service integration and management.

In addition, there is a wealth of service management information available – including academic research and formal standards related to services and service management, such as ISO/IEC 20000, as well as blogs, forums and other more informal content.

Service management has developed as IT's focus has moved from a technology-centric approach to an end-to-end service and value-based approach. The ITIL 4 approach focuses on the consumer and the quality of service the consumer receives. IT is increasingly seen as a vital business enabler, and IT plans must be aligned to overall business models, strategies and plans.

Another factor that has contributed to the advancement and development of service management is the increasing complexity of service delivery. More and more organisations are using shared services or have outsourced some or all IT provision to external organisations. As the number of stakeholders involved with service delivery increases, more sophisticated service management is required to control them. As supply chains get more complex, service management practices need to adapt. The increased complexity of delivery has strengthened and improved service management, as well as imposing greater challenges.

Organisation

Organisations facilitate value creation. The definition of an organisation is:

> *"A person or a group of people that has its own functions with responsibilities, authorities, and relationships to achieve its objectives".*

An organisation could be:

- A single person;

- A team within an organisation;
- A legal entity (a company, or a charity); or
- A government department or public-sector body.

Note that an organisation can be a single person – for example, a sole trader. Within this definition, an organisation does not have to be a legal entity. It could be a team that interacts with other teams inside the same legal entity (for example, the IT department provides services to the marketing department).

It's important to define what the term 'organisation' refers to so that relationships can be identified and managed. For example, some businesses expect their IT department to behave like an external service provider organisation and to transact with the other business departments as customer organisations. Other businesses define themselves as a single organisation and see all of their internal departments working together as part of the whole organisation. There is no right or wrong way to structure these relationships, but they do need to be defined and managed.

Historically, some organisations did not listen to their customers. They saw their relationship with customers as being:

- One-directional
- Distant
- Without feedback

In fact, value is a two-way relationship. Value is co-created, a term that implies involvement from both the service provider organisation and the consumer.

The growth of online services allows organisations to capture feedback from their customers much more easily.

For example, in the past, a new piece of software may have been released every 12 months, based on an aggregated set of feedback and updated requirements. Now, service provider organisations can track what buttons customers are clicking, how long they spend on a page and even where their eyes are moving. They can release software more frequently – perhaps many times a day – to respond to the feedback they have been monitoring.

Co-creation

Co-creation focuses on customer experience and interactive relationships. It encourages active customer involvement. Organisations need to collaborate with their customers and consumers, as well as the suppliers that help them to offer valuable services. Each product and service is part of a web of service relationships. Most organisations act as a customer and a service provider as part of service delivery: buying and selling or consuming and supplying services and service elements.

For value co-creation to take place, both the consumer and the service provider organisation must get value from the product or service.

For example, consider using a travel agent to book a holiday. The outcome that you (the consumer) want is the holiday of a lifetime, and the travel agent (the service provider organisation) will help you achieve this. You need to share information about your budget, desired location, activities, planned dates, etc. The travel agent will then provide you with options tailored to your requirements. They will use other service provider organisations like hotels, airlines and transfer companies to build the service for you. Together, you will create the value you want from your trip. If you, as the consumer, withhold important information from the travel agent, they are unlikely to be able to meet your needs. You receive value as the consumer, but the travel agent also receives value, perhaps through profit, repeat business and your word-of-mouth recommendations.

CHAPTER 2: SERVICE MANAGEMENT ROLES

In this chapter, we look at some of the service management roles and relationships that need to be defined and managed by organisations. These include:

- Service provider
- Stakeholder
- Service relationship
- Consumer
  - Customer
  - User
  - Sponsor
- Stakeholders and value types

Some role considerations

Roles are carried out by people and need to be clearly defined so that those people understand what they are supposed to do. Clear roles and responsibilities are essential for an effective service management organisation. If roles are not clear, tasks may be duplicated – or not done at all.

Remember: a single person can fulfil many roles – that's why it is so important to map roles carefully.

Many organisations that are new to ITIL and service management look at all the ITIL practices and panic. They think they need to hire hundreds of new staff to fulfil all the roles – confusing a job or person with a role.

In a smaller organisation, one person may have lots of roles. ITIL doesn't mean hiring lots of staff, but simply means matching the service management roles with the existing IT staff members. For example, one staff member might carry out change enablement and configuration management roles. Service desk staff might have roles within incident management, access management and request fulfilment.

Service provider

The organisation delivering a service is acting as a service provider. A service provider can be part of the same organisation as a consumer (for example, an IT department offering services to a sales team), or an external organisation (for example, a software solutions provider selling to customers).

A service provider organisation must understand who its customers or consumers are, and which other stakeholders are part of its wider service relationships.

There is still a common perception that ITIL is only suitable for organisations of certain sizes or in certain sectors, but this is not the case. Every IT service provider organisation, for example, needs change enablement of some type. The type and size of the organisation will influence how change enablement is implemented, but the underlying reason for having change enablement (protecting services while delivering new or updated functionality) remains the same.

Stakeholder

A stakeholder is *"a person or organization that has an interest or involvement in an organization, product, service, practice, or other entity"*.

Stakeholders can be anyone – internal or external to the organisation.

If a service provider organisation doesn't understand what its consumers want, it has no chance of being able to deliver services to meet their needs. The organisation needs to build relationships with stakeholders to improve communication and really get to know them and their requirements. It is important to remember that the term 'stakeholder' covers more than just consumers. Examples of stakeholders could also include:

- Suppliers and partners
- Shareholders and investors
- Auditors
- Employees

There are many techniques available for stakeholder mapping; if this is an area where your organisation could improve, an Internet search will yield much useful information.

Service relationship

A service relationship is *"a co-operation between a service provider and a service consumer. Service relationships include service provision, service consumption, and service relationship management."*

Changing our perspective from 'making a sale' to managing a relationship can have a big impact on how we behave as a service provider organisation. When an organisation is new or immature, it will chase every single customer it can possibly find, even if that customer may be difficult to work with or even toxic. More mature organisations recognise that there are some customers with which they do not want to work, because the overhead of managing the relationship outweighs the benefits of the initial sale.

Managing service relationships requires the service provider organisation to continue to allocate time and resources after a purchase has been made or a service has been provided. Automation can help with this process; for example, you might receive a reminder when your automobile insurance or health insurance is due for renewal, along with an enquiry about whether anything has changed.

Effective service relationship management brings benefits for both the service provider organisation and the consumer. The service provider can have confidence that its customers will be loyal, allowing it to invest in its services and take a long-term planning view. The consumer will feel that they are being listened to and should be confident that the service will continue to meet their needs.

Service consumer

The service consumer is the person or organisation receiving a service. Most organisations will act as service providers and service consumers as part of normal service delivery (for example, as a consumer they buy components to build a service they supply as a service provider). Consumer is a broad term that includes customer, user and sponsor.

Table 1: The Service Consumer

Customer	*"The role that defines the requirements for a service and takes responsibility for the outcomes of service consumption."*
User	*"The role that uses services."*
Sponsor	*"The role that authorizes budget for service consumption. Can also be used to describe an organization or individual that provides financial or other support for an initiative."*

One individual might act as the customer, the user and the sponsor for a service (for example, an individual who enters into a mobile phone contract fulfils all of these roles). In other situations, the roles are held by separate people (for example, a purchasing department procures mobile phones for staff in a sales team).

Defining roles clearly supports:

- Better communication;
- Better relationships; and
- Better stakeholder management.

The roles within the 'consumer' definition can have different and conflicting expectations about value, agreeing essential requirements, and how much they are prepared to pay. For example, consider a project to provide new laptops to a team of mobile sales representatives:

- The sponsor works in procurement and has little understanding of the sales role. Its goal is to purchase the cheapest laptops possible.

- The customer is the sales team leader, who wants the team to be happy but has been office-based for some years, so has lost sight of mobile workers' requirements.
- The users are the sales representatives who will receive the laptops, and they are likely to be unhappy as their needs have not been recognised.

In this scenario, it would be better for the users to be active in the customer role as well, so that the requirements are clearly defined up front.

Different stakeholders receive different types of value.

Table 2: Examples of Stakeholder and Value Types

Stakeholder	Value example
Service consumer	Receives benefits from the service, and optimises the costs and risks it incurs related to it.
Service provider	Receives funding or loyalty from consumers, supporting further business development and reputation enhancement.
Service provider employees	Job satisfaction, financial and non-financial rewards, personal development.
Society and community	Employment, taxes, corporate social responsibility initiatives.

Charity organisations	Financial and non-financial contributions.
Shareholders	Financial benefits, such as dividends.

Using RACI models for role mapping

The RACI (Responsible, Accountable, Consulted and Informed) model is used to track who is doing what. It provides clear mapping of roles across the different teams in the organisational structure.

RACI models are used to manage resources and roles for the delivery of a piece of work or task. Resources can be drawn from different functional areas within an organisation, which makes it challenging for line managers to track what their staff are doing. For example, a technical resource might be involved with incident investigation, problem resolution, a project and working with a new supplier.

Only one person can be **Accountable** for any task. The person who is accountable for the task has the overall authority for the task – but they may not carry out individual pieces of work themselves.

Any number of people can be **Responsible** as part of the RACI model. These are the workers who will get the actual tasks done, and they will report to the **Accountable** resource about their progress.

Sometimes resources are **Consulted** to get a task done. This might be a person within the organisation who has specific knowledge, or it could be a document store, or even an Internet search engine. These resources need to be tracked to ensure they are available when required.

Other resources need to be **Informed**. These are stakeholders who need to track and understand exactly how the task is proceeding, or they may need an output from the task. Business sponsors, for example, will typically be informed about progress as part of a project.

When RACI is applied to service management processes, the process owner will be accountable for all the process activities, even if they are not responsible for carrying them out.

RACI models are often shown as a matrix. To build a RACI matrix, these steps need to be followed:

- Identify activities.
- Identify roles.
- Assign RACI codes.
- Identify gaps or overlaps.
- Distribute the matrix for feedback.
- Monitor the roles.

Have a go: why not draw your own RACI matrix? You can also find many examples on the Internet. Table 3, below, shows an example of a RACI matrix for a coffee shop making a customer's coffee order. Notice how someone is accountable for every task.

Table 3: A Simple RACI matrix

Fulfilling a coffee order	Customer	Store owner	Staff member	Supplier
Providing staff		A	R/C	
Providing premises		A	R	

2: Service management roles

		A	C	R
Providing ingredients		A	C	R
Providing order details	A/C		R/I	
Making and delivering coffee	C/I		A/R	
Confirmation of order fulfilment	I		A/R	
Drinking and approving coffee	A/R	I	I	

CHAPTER 3: ALL ABOUT SERVICES

This chapter defines:

- Products and services
- Utility
- Warranty
- Output
- Outcome
- Risk

📋 Products and services

The services an organisation provides are based on one or more products. Products are created from configurations of the resources to which an organisation has access. Resources include:

- People
- Information
- Technology
- Value streams
- Processes
- Suppliers
- Partners

"A product is a configuration of an organization's resources designed to offer value for a consumer."

"A service is a means of enabling value co-creation, by facilitating outcomes that customers want to achieve,

without the customer having to manage specific costs and risks."

Service provider organisations need to consider the following areas to assess whether or not they are delivering value:

- Cost
- Risk
- Outputs
- Outcomes
- Utility
- Warranty

Service provider organisations need to balance the areas listed above to deliver attractive services. For example, a free online banking service might be attractive to consumers, but if it is insecure and risky, they will quickly stop using it. Free one-hour delivery for items ordered via a website could also be attractive but might be too costly for the organisation to continue offering. Products and services need to be considered holistically; too much focus on one element of a product or a service could mean the 'big picture' is missed and the customer doesn't get the outcome they wanted.

Outputs and outcomes

A service provider organisation produces outputs, which help its consumers achieve their desired outcomes. This is where co-creation is important; without input or activity from the consumer, no value is created.

"An output is a tangible or intangible deliverable of an activity."

"An outcome is a result for a stakeholder enabled by one or more outputs."

Value is created when a service has more positive than negative effects. For example, it might cost a consumer money to pay for an externally provided email service, but it reduces the amount of money the consumer spends on internal resources and transfers the risks associated with hardware failure to another organisation. Figure 1 shows the balance between the costs and risks removed or introduced by a service.

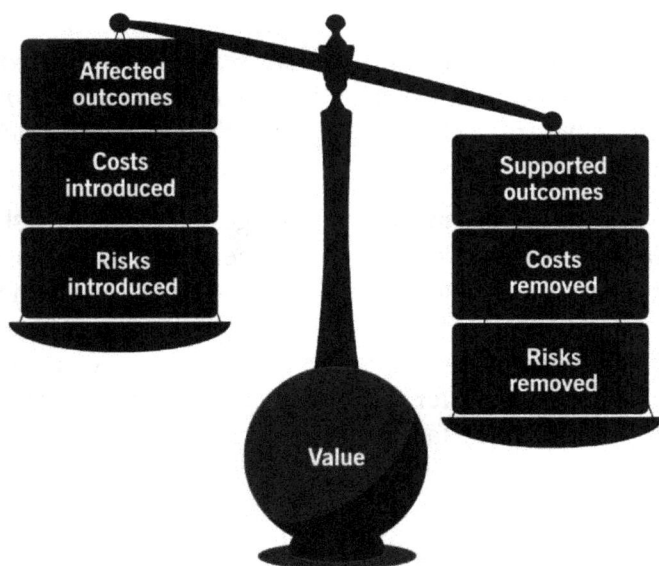

Figure 1: Achieving value: outcomes, costs and risks[2]

---

[2] *ITIL® Foundation, ITIL 4 edition*, figure 2.2.

3: All about services

The service provider organisation needs to understand the costs of service provision to make sure they are within set budgetary constraints and the organisation is profitable, where relevant. For example, public-sector organisations might be required to meet budget targets rather than generate a profit.

Cost and risk

Cost is *"the amount of money spent on a specific activity or resource"*.

Risk is *"a possible event that could cause harm or loss or make it difficult to achieve objectives. Risk can also be defined as uncertainty of outcome and can be used in the context of measuring the probability of positive outcomes as well as negative outcomes"*.

Service provider organisations manage the detail of risk on behalf of the consumer. The consumer participates in risk reduction by helping to define the service, and what it needs to do. For example, think about an online file storage service. There is a range of security options that the service provider organisation can offer, from minimal security to full encryption and multi-factor authentication. More complexity will add more cost for the service provider, so the consumer's attitude to risk must be understood for the service to be designed appropriately.

Utility and warranty

Service provider organisations assess the utility and warranty of a service to check it will create value.

- Utility describes what the service does (is it fit for purpose?)
- Warranty describes how the service performs (is it fit for use?)

"Utility is the functionality offered by a product or service to meet a particular need."

This describes what the service does and whether it is fit for purpose. A service can provide utility by removing constraints from the consumer, or supporting their performance, or both.

"Warranty is the assurance that a product or service will meet agreed requirements."

Warranty describes how a service performs, and whether it is fit for use. Warranty covers areas like availability, capacity, security and continuity; the service must meet the levels required by the consumer.

For example, consider a social media platform. Utility requirements could include:

- Allowing users to 'follow' accounts they are interested in;
- Allowing users to decide if they want to see the most recent or most popular content; and
- Allowing users to 'block' accounts with which they do not want to interact.

Warranty requirements could include:

- The platform is available when users want to access it (for example, it doesn't fail because of high traffic);
- The platform keeps users' details secure; and

- The platform could be restored if there were a major issue.

Cost, risk, utility and warranty all provide a picture of a service's viability.

CHAPTER 4: SERVICE RELATIONSHIPS

This chapter explains service relationships in more detail, including:

- Service offerings
- Service relationship management
- Service provision
- Service consumption

Service offerings

"A service offering is a description of one or more services, designed to address the needs of a target consumer group. A service offering may include goods, access to resources, and service actions."

Table 4: Service Offerings

Goods	With goods, ownership is transferred to the consumer; for example, buying a car. The consumer takes responsibility for future use of the goods.
Access to resources	With access to resources, ownership is not transferred to the consumer; for example, renting a car. Access is granted or licensed under agreed terms and conditions; for example, the consumer might agree not to drive more than 10,000 miles per year.

Service actions	Service actions are performed by the provider to address a consumer need; for example, roadside assistance if a car breaks down. They are performed according to the agreement with the consumer; for example, paying extra to have guaranteed assistance within one hour.

The consumer groups to which a service is offered may be part of the same organisation as the service provider, or they might be external to the service provider. Service providers can offer the same product in different ways to different consumer groups; for example, short-term or long-term car leases, or leases with a right-to-buy at the end of the lease.

Service relationships

"A service relationship is a cooperation between a service provider and a service consumer. Service relationships include service provision, service consumption, and service relationship management."

Table 5: Service Relationships

Service provision	*"Activities performed by an organization to provide services. This includes management of resources configured to deliver the service, access to these resources for users, fulfilment of agreed service actions, service performance management and continual improvement. It may also include the supply of goods."*

Service consumption	*"Activities performed by an organization to consume services. This includes the management of the consumer's resources needed to use the service, service use actions performed by users, and may include receiving (acquiring) goods."*
Service relationship management	*"This includes joint activities performed by a service provider and a service consumer to ensure continual value co-creation based on agreed and available service offerings."*

Figure 2 shows a generic representation of a service. You could use this figure to map some of your own organisation's services and assess how they are offered to consumers.

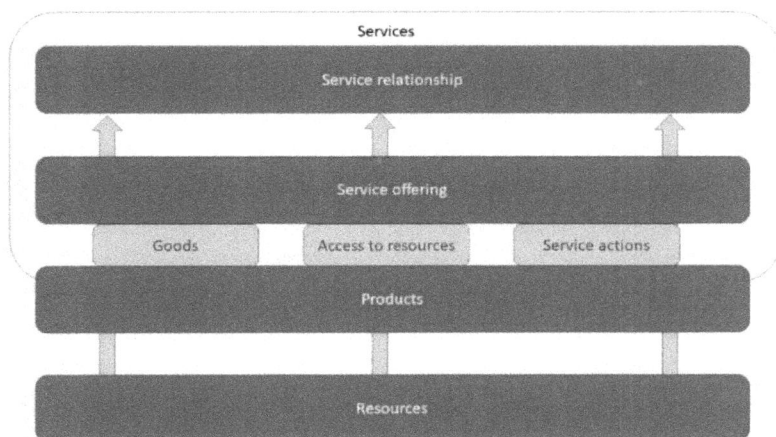

Figure 2: A generic representation of a service

The service relationship model

Figure 3 shows the service relationship model.[3]

---

[3] *ITIL® Foundation, ITIL 4 edition*, figure 2.1.

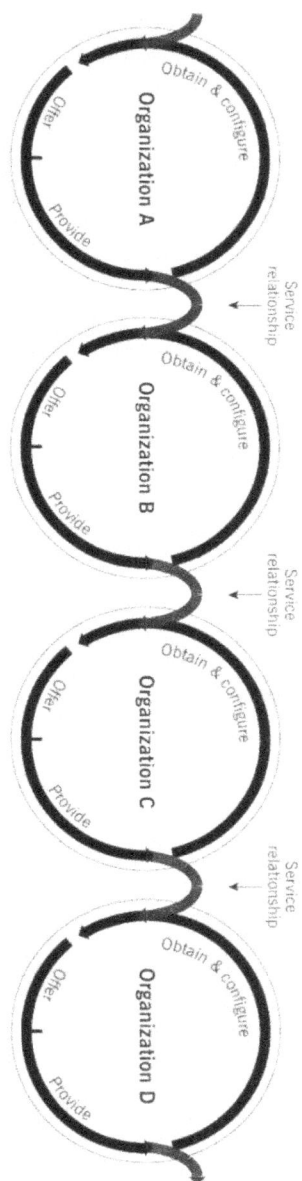

Figure 3: The service relationship model

In this figure, services delivered by Organisation A create or modify resources within Organisation B. Organisation B can then use these resources to provide services to its own consumers. For example, laptop manufacturer Organisation B buys chips from Organisation A as part of its production process. It sells its laptops to Organisation C, which gives them to its consultants.

This figure shows a supply and consumption chain, but remember that for most organisations, supply and consumption is a more complex network of relationships.

CHAPTER 5: THE FOUR DIMENSIONS OF SERVICE MANAGEMENT

The four dimensions are:

- Organisations and people
- Information and technology
- Partners and suppliers
- Value streams and processes

The four dimensions of service management are relevant to all elements of the Service Value System (see chapter 6). Failing to consider all four dimensions can lead to services that offer poor quality or efficiency, or may even mean services aren't delivered at all. The four dimensions can overlap and interact in unpredictable ways and must be considered for every service. Figure 4 shows the four dimensions[4]:

---

[4] *ITIL® Foundation, ITIL 4 edition*, figure 3.1.

The four dimensions of service management

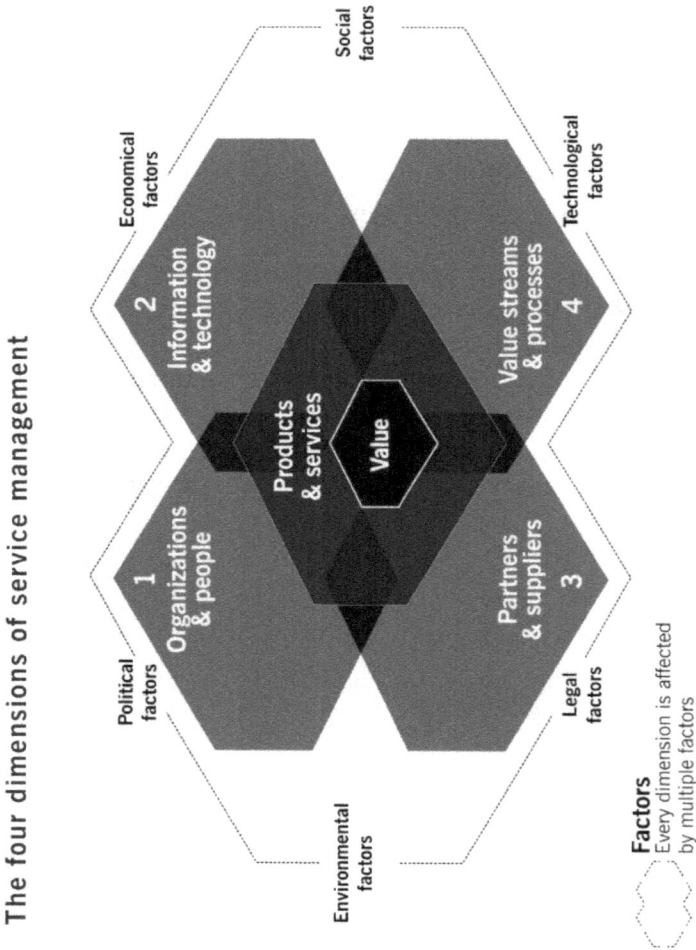

Figure 4: The four dimensions of service management

The factors on the edge of the figure can all affect or constrain any of the four dimensions. For example, legal factors might limit in which country an organisation can store information. Any factor can affect any dimension. The factors are based on PESTEL (or PESTLE), a framework used to assess macro-environmental factors.

🌍 PESTEL is often used within business analysis, and assesses the environment an organisation, product or service is operating in and the impact it can have. PESTEL is described in more detail in Table 6.

Table 6: PESTEL

Political	How might political or government actions affect an organisation, product or service? For example, consider the impact of legislation on organisations like Uber and Airbnb.
Economic	Will national or global economic performance affect a product, service or organisation? For example, a recession might mean that consumers are less willing to purchase some types of service.
Social	What is the social environment of the market? Do cultural trends have any impact? For example, seasonal events like religious and public holidays.
Technological	Are there any innovations in technology that could have an impact? Many new

	technologies such as artificial intelligence, robotic process automation, etc. have yet to reach their full potential.
Environmental	These factors can include climate, weather, geographical location, etc. For example, a mild winter might leave a clothes retailer with large numbers of unsold coats.
Legal	What legislation and regulations affect an organisation, product or service? What policies does an organisation have internally? This can include areas like health and safety legislation.

Not considering any of the four dimensions can lead to reduced value or no value at all. For example, an organisation might focus too much on technology and neglect the people who are going to use it, leading to no value being delivered.

Dimension 1: Organizations & people

"The complexity of organizations is growing, and it is important to ensure that the way an organization is structured and managed, as well as its roles, responsibilities, and systems of authority and communication, is well defined and supports its overall strategy and operating model."

The scope of organisations and people include:

- Formal organisational structures
- Culture

- Required staffing and competencies (skills)
- Roles and responsibilities

Culture is an essential part of an organisation's success or failure. Considerations include:

- Trust
- Transparency
- Collaboration and shared values
- Leaders who champion values
- Coordination

Some of the areas that organisations need to consider as part of this dimension include:

- Management and leadership styles
- Updating skills and competencies
- Communication and collaboration
- Broad knowledge plus deep specialisation
- Common objectives
- Breaking down silos

Organisational structure describes how roles and responsibilities are allocated and coordinated within an organisation: who does what, who reports to who, and how. Most organisations have adopted one of the following approaches to departmentalisation:

- Functional structure: activities are grouped by their skills, e.g. Sales, Customer Services or Finance.
- Divisional structure: activities are grouped by customer region, product or service, e.g. EMEA team, online banking versus retail banking, etc.

- Matrix structure: a combination of functional and divisional, e.g. a finance expert might work on an online banking project as an advisor.

Within the organisational structure, employees might also experience:

- Formal or informal management: how much of their role is governed by explicit rules and regulations?
- Centralised or decentralised management: what percentage of decisions are taken by a centralised team?
- Tall or flat structures: with more or fewer levels of management and hierarchy.

The type of structure an organisation adopts will depend on its environment, strategy, history, and more. There is no right or wrong structure, but it is important to ensure that it supports organisational objectives. For example, an organisation that wants to innovate quickly might struggle if it has a formal, centralised management structure. It will not be able to attract the type of employees it wants, and existing employees will find it hard to drive innovation because of the amount of approval needed for any new ideas or changes.

Dimension 2: Information & technology

"When applied to the Service Value System, the information and technology dimension includes the information and knowledge necessary for the management of services, as well as the technologies required. It also incorporates the relationships between different components of the Service Value System, such as the inputs and outputs of activities and practices."

Organisations need to consider:

- What information is managed by the services?
- What supporting information and knowledge are needed to deliver and manage the services?
- How will the information and knowledge assets be protected, managed, archived and disposed of?

Technology that supports IT-enabled services includes:

- IT architecture
- Databases
- Blockchain
- Cognitive computing
- Applications (including mobile applications)
- Communication systems
- Artificial intelligence
- Cloud computing

Technology that supports ITSM includes:

- Workflow management
- Communication systems
- Inventory systems
- Mobile platforms
- Cloud solutions
- Knowledge bases
- Analytical tools
- Remote collaboration
- Artificial intelligence
- Machine learning

Many IT-enabled services rely on effective information management to deliver value (for example, customer loyalty schemes or Cloud storage for photos). Information management includes the areas shown in Table 7.

Table 7: Terms Related to Information Management

Availability	*"The ability of an IT service or other configuration item to perform its agreed function when required."*
Reliability	*"The ability of a product, service or other configuration item to perform its intended function for a specified period of time or number of cycles."*
Accessibility	Accessibility includes making sure information is only available to those who should have access to it along with designing for all consumers, including those with disabilities.
Timeliness	Is information available at an appropriate or useful time?
Accuracy	Is information accurate?
Relevance	Is information relevant?

'Digital transformation' is a term used to describe how information technology now underpins every area of business activity. Think about your own role (and, indeed, your personal life). How reliant are you on technology? As the importance of information technology grows, so do the risks associated with it. You've probably read news stories about organisations that have suffered a data or security breach. These cyber security incidents can have both financial and reputational consequences.

AXELOS, the owner of ITIL, has published RESILIA™ to help meet these challenges. RESILIA is described as "a comprehensive portfolio of tools and training to help your organization achieve global best practice in cyber security. RESILIA helps embed best practice cyber security skills and behaviors throughout your organization, regardless of employees' roles or responsibilities. With RESILIA you can move beyond effective cyber security and achieve cyber resilience."

Dimension 3: Partners & suppliers

"The partners and suppliers dimension encompasses an organization's relationships with other organizations that are involved in the design, development, deployment, delivery, support and/or continual improvement of services. It also incorporates contracts and other agreements between the organization and its partners or suppliers."

The scope of the partners and suppliers dimension includes:

- Service provider/service consumer relationships;
- An organisation's partner and supplier strategy;
- Factors that influence supplier strategies; and
- Service integration and management (SIAM).

Supplier and partner relationships range from simple, commodity services to complex partnerships with shared goals and risks. Very few organisations operate completely independently and use no services from other organisations.

Table 8: Service Integration and Management

Service integration and management	As organisations rely on more and more suppliers, it can prove challenging to manage them, particularly when things go wrong. SIAM is a management methodology that uses a service integrator role to coordinate service relationships across all suppliers. Service integration and management might be carried out by staff within the organisation or by an external organisation.

Figure 5 shows how the service integrator role sits between service provider organisations and the commissioning (customer) organisation.

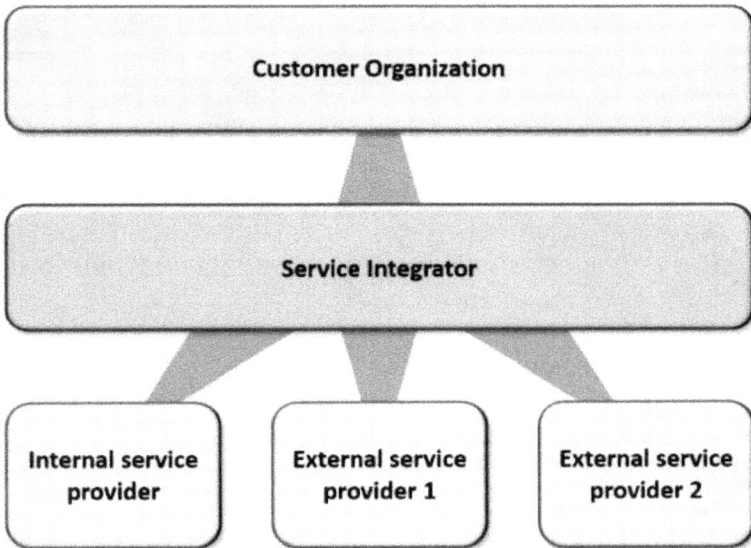

Figure 5: The SIAM ecosystem[5]

Table 9 explains the factors that can affect an organisation's supplier strategy.

---

[5] *Service Integration and Management Foundation Body of Knowledge, Scopism Limited, 2017.*

Table 9: Factors Affecting Supplier Strategy

Strategic focus	Some organisations value self-sufficiency, whereas others prefer to outsource non-core work.
Corporate culture	Cultural bias can influence sourcing decisions, perhaps based on previous bad experiences.
Resource scarcity	Some resources and skills are hard to find, forcing an organisation to source them externally.
Cost concerns	It may be cheaper to source services externally, e.g. using shared resources to provide 24x7 support.
Subject matter expertise	Suppliers can bring deep expertise that the organisation cannot build internally.
External constraints	Legislation and regulation can affect sourcing decisions.
Demand patterns	Organisations might use external suppliers to help them cope with spikes in demand, e.g. using seasonal staff to provide extra support during holiday periods.

The importance of external suppliers in service delivery affects the skills that an ITSM professional needs. Instead of creating a product or service, the ITSM professional might be involved with contract negotiation and agreement. Instead of carrying out activities, they might be overseeing a supplier and managing the ongoing relationship. Commercial issues are more likely to arise if suppliers are chosen and contracts agreed by a procurement team that has little or no contact with the product or service teams. A procurement team might be very price-driven, leading to a contract that delivers an unacceptable level of quality. ITSM professionals need to be able to work across silos to make sure the contracts agreed meet desired outcomes.

Dimension 4: Value streams & processes

"Applied to the organization and its Service Value System, the value streams and processes dimension is concerned with how the various parts of the organization work in an integrated and coordinated way to enable value creation through products and services. The dimension focuses on what activities the organization undertakes and how they are organized, as well as how the organization ensures that it is enabling value creation for all stakeholders efficiently and effectively."

A value stream is *"a series of steps an organization undertakes to create and deliver products and services to consumers"*.

Value streams and processes define the activities, workflows, controls and procedures needed to achieve agreed objectives. The scope of this dimension includes:

- Activities the organisation undertakes;

- How activities are organised; and
- How value creation is ensured for all stakeholders efficiently and effectively.

An organisation needs to understand its value streams to improve its overall performance. Organisations will:

- Examine work and map value streams
- Analyse streams and steps to identify waste
- Eliminate waste
- Identify improvements
- Continually optimise value streams

Value stream mapping has many benefits. Without an understanding of its value streams, an organisation is unable to explain, measure or improve them.

One benefit of value stream mapping that achieves improvements quickly is the ability to identify bottlenecks; in other words, an activity, area or process that is impeding flow. We'll use a simple value stream to illustrate this.

An organisation is mapping its value stream for the deployment of customer relationship management software to sales team members. Sales staff are complaining that the process is too slow and the delay is stopping them carrying out their roles effectively. The organisation decides to map the value stream and try to identify the bottlenecks. The steps it follows are to:

- Identify all the activities and steps in the process;
- Record the average time it takes to complete each step and the average wait time between each step;

- Map this on a simple diagram showing value add times (time to complete each step) and wait times between steps; and
- Identify the delays that can be reduced, perhaps using the longest delay or the one that is the simplest to fix.

The mapping activity produces the value stream shown in Figure 6.

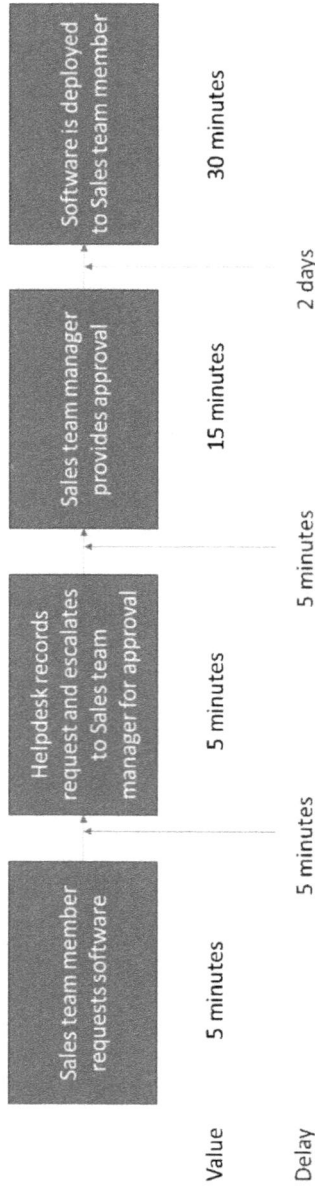

Figure 6: A simple value stream

Note where the longest delay is: between the approval and the deployment. Perhaps some automation could help here?

📋 The key message for processes is:

"A process is a set of activities that transforms inputs into outputs. Processes describe what is done to accomplish an objective, and well-defined processes can improve productivity within and across organizations. They are usually detailed in procedures, which outline who is involved in the process, and work instructions, which explain how they are carried out."

A process is a set of interrelated or interacting activities that transforms inputs into outputs. Processes are designed to accomplish a specific objective. Figure 7 shows a simple example:

Figure 7: A simple process

🌐 The word 'process' has acquired some negative connotations within an IT environment. Within the DevOps community, previous versions of ITIL have sometimes been seen as bureaucratic, process-driven models that can impede flow and stop work getting done. Some organisations did treat ITIL v3 as a process 'catalogue' and made it their mission to implement the full set, exactly as described in the books.

It's important to focus on having 'just enough' process to get the job done. Too much process can create barriers (and lead to people avoiding a process altogether), but having no process at all can lead to chaos. Each organisation needs to adopt and adapt processes to help it meet its own organisational goals, and review processes regularly to ensure they are still efficient and effective. The updates in the ITIL 4 guidance and the focus on practices aim to revise this perception.

Value streams and processes for products and services help define:

- What is the generic delivery model for the service, and how does the service work?
- What are the value streams involved in delivering the agreed outputs of the service?
- Who, or what, performs the required service actions?

CHAPTER 6: THE SERVICE VALUE SYSTEM

The ITIL Service Value System (SVS) is *"a model representing how all the components and activities of an organization work together to facilitate value creation"*.

It includes:

- Guiding principles
- Governance
- Service value chain
- Practices
- Continual improvement
- Inputs and outcomes

"The ITIL SVS describes how all the components and activities of an organization work together as a system to enable value creation. Each organization's SVS has interfaces with other organizations, forming an ecosystem that can, in turn, facilitate value for those organizations, their customers, and their stakeholders."

Figure 8 shows the SVS[6]:

---

[6] *ITIL® Foundation, ITIL 4 edition*, figure 4.1.

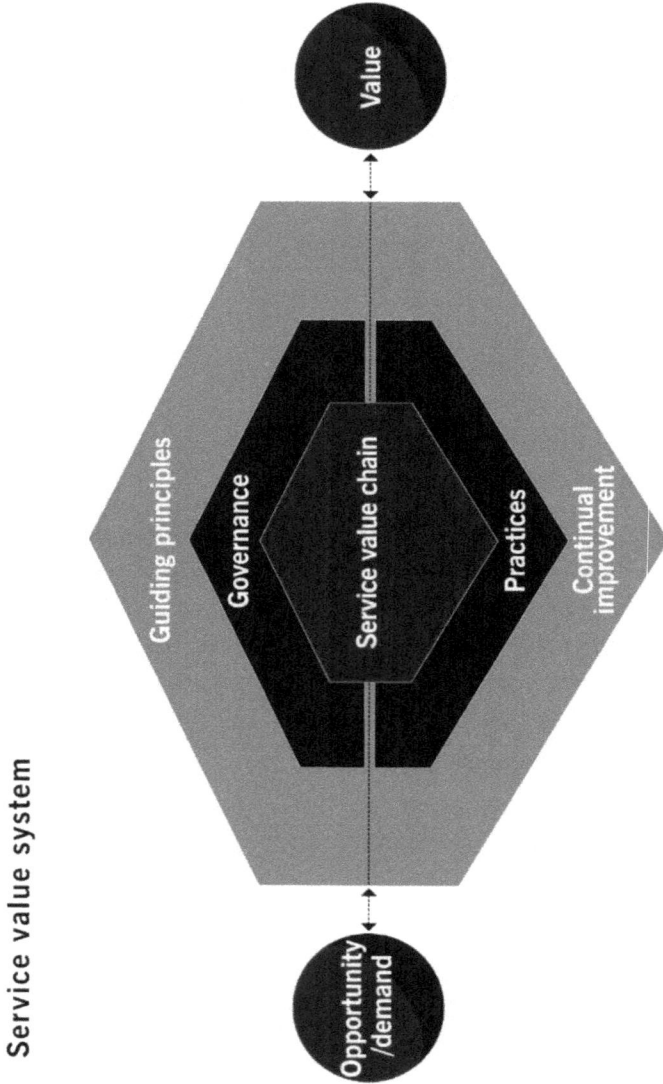

Figure 8: The ITIL Service Value System

Table 10 further explains the elements of the SVS:

Table 10: Elements of the SVS

Opportunity/ demand	Opportunities represent options or possibilities to add value for stakeholders or otherwise improve the organisation. Demand is the need or desire for products and services that originates from internal and external consumers. Opportunity and demand are inputs to the SVS.
Value	The outcome of the SVS is value. The SVS can enable the creation of different types of value for different stakeholders.
Guiding principles	The guiding principles are recommendations that can guide an organisation in all circumstances, regardless of changes in goals, strategies, types of work or management structure. The guiding principles are a component of the SVS.
Governance	Governance is the means by which an organisation is directed and controlled. Governance activities include evaluate, direct and monitor. Governance is an element of the SVS.
Service value chain	The service value chain is a set of interconnected activities that an organisation performs to deliver a

	valuable product or service to its consumers and to facilitate value realisation. The service value chain is an element of the SVS.
Practices	The ITIL practices are sets of organisational resources designed for performing work or accomplishing an objective. Practices are an element of the SVS.
Continual improvement	Continual improvement is a recurring organisational activity performed at all levels to ensure that an organisation's performance is always aligned to changing stakeholder expectations. Continual improvement is an element of the SVS.

The SVS is designed to combat silos within an organisation. Silos exist when teams or departments focus solely on their own areas of work or influence, ignoring the 'big picture' and not looking across the organisation holistically. Silos make it more difficult for an organisation to become agile and resilient, because they limit effective communication and reduce the power of a shared vision. A siloed organisation will experience these symptoms:

- Inability to act quickly or take advantage of opportunities.

- Reduced ability to optimise resource use across the organisation.
- Poor decision making.
- Poor visibility/a lack of transparency.
- Hidden agendas and an increase in unhealthy organisational politics.
- A lack of clarity about value streams, interfaces and handoff points.

Looking at the organisation from the value system perspective helps to discourage silos. The value chain activities and practices are not a fixed or rigid structure; instead, they are configured into value streams to meet the needs of the organisation and can be reconfigured as those needs change. The value system provides a structure that enables flexibility.

In the next chapters we will study the elements of the SVS:

- Opportunity, demand, value
- Guiding principles
- Governance
- Service value chain
- Practices (including continual improvement)

Value is created by the SVS; this will not be studied in more detail and has already been covered as a concept in earlier chapters.

CHAPTER 7: THE SVS: OPPORTUNITY, DEMAND, VALUE

"Opportunity and demand trigger activities within the ITIL Service Value System (SVS) and these activities lead to the creation of value. Opportunity and demand are always entering into the system, but the organization does not automatically accept all opportunities or satisfy all demand."

Opportunities are ways a service provider organisation might be able to add value for stakeholders or somehow improve their own organisation. Organisations will always need to balance the time and resources they allocate to new or changed services against the time and resources they allocate to improvement opportunities. Too much focus on just one area will lead to problems in the longer term. For example, an organisation that only focuses on improving existing services might find itself unprepared for a major change in its market. An organisation that only focuses on new services might find its existing services are neglected and its customer base becomes unhappy.

How do we identify opportunities? This is a crucial question for a service provider organisation. There are many different strategic tools and techniques that can be used to help provide an answer.

One such technique is the 'blue ocean/red ocean' approach. A red ocean is defined as an established market with entrenched industry practices and intense competition. A blue ocean is an untapped market space, free of competition, where an organisation can create customers. The blue ocean has the potential to provide rapid growth and large profits. Identifying the 'blue ocean' for a service provider organisation can help to identify where resources will be best allocated.

We could reasonably expect our customers to tell us what they want, which creates opportunities, but this isn't always simple, particularly in the technology market space. What if our customers can't imagine how technology can help them? As Henry Ford famously said of motor cars, "If I had asked people what they wanted, they would have said faster horses." For digital or information technology service provider organisations, part of their ongoing service relationship management priorities will be to help their customers imagine the impossible and appreciate how technology can help them.

Equally, not every idea we receive from our customers is a good one. What people believe they want – and what they actually need – can be very different things. If a service provider organisation sees an opportunity but isn't sure that demand truly exists, it needs to allocate resources very carefully. Agile development describes the use of a minimum viable product (MVP) to provide feedback for future product development. An MVP has just enough features to satisfy early customers and can help to identify any incorrect assumptions that have been made. This reduces the cost and risk associated with the development project. The MVP process can also include carrying out market analysis before any development actually takes place. The MVP will:

- Allow a product hypothesis to be tested;
- Use minimal resources;
- Accelerate learning;
- Get the product or service to customers as soon as possible; and
- Provide an opportunity for feedback for future development.

CHAPTER 8: THE SVS: GUIDING PRINCIPLES

A guiding principle is a *"recommendation that guides an organization in all circumstances"*.

Many things change in day-to-day operations:

- Goals
- Key staff
- Strategies
- Types of work
- Management and organisational structure

Guiding principles remain constant, no matter what else changes. Using guiding principles allows organisations to integrate multiple ways of working and management methods within service management. For example, some organisations follow a waterfall way of working, while others use methods like Agile and DevOps. The principles allow different ways of working to be used, while making sure appropriate outcomes are delivered.

Table 11: Waterfall, Agile and DevOps

Waterfall	*"Waterfall is a development approach that is linear and sequential with distinct objectives for each phase of development."*
Agile	*"Agile is an umbrella term for a collection of frameworks and techniques that together enable teams and individuals to work in a way that is typified by collaboration,*

	prioritization, iterative and incremental delivery and timeboxing. There are specific methods (or frameworks) that are classed as Agile, such as Scrum, Lean and Kanban."
DevOps	*"DevOps is an organizational culture that aims to improve the flow of value to customers. DevOps focuses on culture, automation, Lean, measurement and sharing (CALMS)."*

The guiding principles should encourage and support continual improvement. They apply across the organisation at all levels and all staff should be aware of them. In each situation, staff and organisations should consider their principles and what is applicable. Not all principles are relevant in every situation, but they all need to be reviewed on each occasion to assess if they are appropriate.

The ITIL guiding principles are:

- Focus on value
- Start where you are
- Progress iteratively with feedback
- Collaborate and promote visibility
- Think and work holistically
- Keep it simple and practical
- Optimise and automate

The ITIL authors recommend putting up posters of the guiding principles in your workplace and meeting rooms to help remind everyone to focus on them. Why not try it?

🗒 Guiding principle 1: Focus on value

"Everything the organization does should link back, directly or indirectly, to value for itself, its customers, and other stakeholders."

Services that offer value are attractive to customers. Services must also offer value to the service provider organisation. 'Focus on value' can include:

- Understanding and identifying the service consumer;
- Understanding the consumer's perspective of value;
- Mapping value to intended outcomes, and understanding these can change over time; and
- Understanding the customer experience (CX) and/or user experience (UX).

Table 12: Customer and User Experience

Customer experience	CX is *"the sum of functional and emotional interactions with a service and service provider as perceived by a service consumer"*.
User experience	UX is the experience of interacting with a product or service focusing on usability and aesthetics (e.g. user interface, touch and feel of the interaction, graphics, content, features,

	ease of use, etc.). Sometimes known as the digital experience (DX).[7]

As part of service provision, organisations need to know:

- Why consumers use services;
- What the services help them to do (the outcomes they support);
- How services help them achieve goals;
- The cost to the consumer; and
- The risks for the consumer.

To successfully apply this principle, service provider organisations need to consider:

- How consumers use each service;
- How to encourage all of their staff to focus on value;
- How to maintain a focus on value in day-to-day operations, not just as an improvement project; and
- How to embed focus on value in every single improvement initiative.

An organisation's employees can only focus on value if they understand what value looks like for their particular organisation as well as its consumers. Does an organisation value profit above everything else? Does it value long-term

---

[7] *VeriSM™: Unwrapped and Applied*, 2018, C. Agutter, J. Botha and S. D. Van Hove, Van Haren Publishing.

customer relationships, or perhaps being seen as an innovator?

In organisations with many layers of management and a hierarchical structure, 'value' might only be understood at senior levels. Frontline workers may be seen as less important and so 'value' isn't communicated to them. Adopting a flatter structure with fewer layers of management can help to communicate key concepts like 'value' to all employees so that they can work effectively.

Guiding principle 2: Start where you are

"In the process of eliminating old, unsuccessful methods or services and creating something better, there can be a great temptation to remove what has been done in the past and build something completely new. This is rarely necessary, or a wise decision. This approach can be extremely wasteful, not only in terms of time, but also in terms of the loss of existing services, processes, people and tools that could have significant value in the improvement effort. Do not start over without first considering what is already available to be leveraged."

Change can be an evolution or a revolution. Revolution is more disruptive and can have unforeseen negative consequences. Before making any change or improvement, it's important to assess the current position and see if anything can be reused or built on.

'Start where you are' can include:

- Assess where you are;
- Observe current services, processes and methods; and

- Use measurements to analyse what is being observed; remember that measuring can affect the results of what is measured.

To apply this principle successfully, service provider organisations need to consider:

- Being as objective as possible about what exists currently;
- Assessing whether current practices and services can/should be replicated or expanded;
- Using risk management skills to support decision making; and
- Recognising that sometimes nothing from the current state can be reused.

🌐 Measurement is described as being particularly important for this principle. What to measure, and how, is a challenge for many organisations.

For IT-enabled products and services, measurement must be considered as part of the design process. It is much more difficult (and often costlier) to try to retrofit measurement after a product or service is live and in use.

Measurement, then, needs to be reviewed continually for usefulness. Are the right people getting the right information to make the right decisions? If not, what needs to change?

Some technical organisations are embracing the concept of 'observability'.

"Observability is achieved when a system is understandable, which is difficult in today's world of increasing software complexity, where most problems are the convergence of many different things failing at once.

One early definition of software observability focused on the three so-called "pillars" of logs, metrics, and traces. That was a good first effort at shifting the priorities of the industry, but the definition is flawed.

A better and more contemporary litmus test for observability is: can you ask the right questions? And can you do it in a way that's predictable, fast, and scalable over time – i.e., without having to re-instrument or launch new code?"[8]

Guiding principle 3: Progress iteratively with feedback

"Resist the temptation to do everything at once. Even huge initiatives must be accomplished iteratively. By organizing work into smaller, manageable sections that can be executed and completed in a timely manner, the focus on each effort will be sharper and easier to maintain."

Feedback can help service provider organisations to understand:

- End-user and customer perception of value;
- The efficiency and effectiveness of their services and value chain;
- The effectiveness of governance and management controls;

---

[8] *www.honeycomb.io/observability/*.

- The interfaces between the organisation and suppliers and partners;
- Demand for products and services; and
- Improvement opportunities, risks and issues.

Working iteratively and using feedback help service provider organisations to be more:

- Flexible;
- Responsive to changing requirements;
- Capable of identifying and responding to failures; and
- Quality-focused.

To successfully apply this principle, service provider organisations need to consider:

- Comprehending the whole, but doing *something*; starting small;
- That the ecosystem is always changing, so feedback is essential; and
- Going fast doesn't mean work is incomplete; iterations may be small, but they are still producing results.

How do we know if feedback is meaningful or accurate? Some service provider organisations dismiss feedback if they feel that it represents a dissatisfied minority. It is true that tools like customer satisfaction surveys are often completed by customers who feel either extremely positive or extremely negative about their experience. Service providers need to follow the basics of statistical sampling and avoid biased sampling techniques.

Guiding principle 4: Collaborate and promote visibility

"When initiatives involve the right people in the correct roles, efforts benefit from better buy-in, more relevance (because better information is available for decision-making) and increased likelihood of long term success."

Collaboration can be viewed as working together towards a shared goal. It can help to remove silos within organisations, allowing everyone to work together more effectively. Collaboration can happen anywhere – inside and outside of the organisation (for example, with other internal teams, or with external suppliers).

Promoting visibility makes work more transparent in the organisation. This helps everyone to:

- Understand what is a priority;
- Balance improvement work and daily work;
- Understand the flow of work;
- Understand where there are bottlenecks; and
- Identify where time, resources and money are being wasted.

To apply this principle successfully, service provider organisations need to consider that:

- Collaboration does not mean consensus; it's not essential that everyone agrees, but everyone must understand why decisions are made;
- Communication must match the audience; different stakeholder groups will need a different message and communication type; and
- Good decisions can only be made when there is visible data to support them.

Collaboration won't just 'happen'. The leaders within a service provider organisation need to create an environment where collaboration can thrive and be rewarded.

Collaboration thrives in high trust environments, which are characterised by:

- Good communication;
- Support between individuals;
- Respect;
- Fairness; and
- Predictability

Think about your own organisation, and whether it is ready for more collaborative working. What might need to change?

Guiding principle 5: Think and work holistically

"No service, practice, process, department or supplier stands alone. The outputs that the organization delivers to itself, its customers and other stakeholders will suffer unless it works in an integrated way to handle its activities as a whole, rather than separate parts. All the organization's activities should be focused on the delivery of value."

To apply this principle successfully, service provider organisations need to consider that:

- The complexity of the system will affect how this principle is applied; higher complexity can create challenges;
- Collaboration supports holistic thinking and working;
- Automation can support holistic working; and

- Patterns in the needs of and interactions between system elements can help identify the holistic viewpoint.

Much recent management thinking has focused on functional specialisation. Value streams are divided into tasks, and resources are directed towards completing one individual task in as near a perfect way as possible. For example, think about a fast-food outlet, with one team member preparing fries, one assembling burgers, one serving customers, etc. This can be highly effective, but also adds a risk that team members lose sight of the big picture. If the team member assembling the burgers decides to save time by leaving out the pickle (thinking that no one likes it anyway!), they create problems for the team member serving customers, who has to deal with complaints.

Think about your own role and your team's role within your organisation. How do you and your team fit into the big picture?

Guiding principle 6: Keep it simple and practical

"Always use the minimum number of steps to accomplish an objective. Outcome-based thinking should be used to produce practical solutions that deliver valuable outcomes."

Processes and services are designed to meet the majority of consumers' needs. Every exception cannot be designed for. It is better to create rules that can be used to handle exceptions when necessary.

To successfully apply this principle, service provider organisations need to:

- Ensure value comes from every activity;
- Recognise that simplicity can be more challenging to create than complexity;
- Do fewer things; do them better;
- Respect people's time; don't make them do unnecessary work;
- Consider that simplicity can support quick wins; and
- Remember that processes or services that are easy to understand are more likely to be used.

In the DevOps community, process is sometimes described as the 'scar tissue' that organisations develop over time (first described by Bridget Kromhout). What this statement describes is the way that an organisation will add extra steps and checks and balances each time something goes wrong, to try to prevent the same situation happening in future. For example, a software patch that has been manually tested might fail in the live environment. In response, an automated test is added and a requirement for sign-off from a test manager. If the patch fails again, sign-off might also be added from a change manager or the application owner. Unintentionally, organisations add complexity to how they work, which can lead to the unintended outcome of employees circumventing the process entirely. This principle is advising us to continually reassess how we work, and look for ways to make things simpler, without compromising value.

Guiding principle 7: Optimize and automate

"Organizations must maximize the value of the work carried out by their human and technical resources. The four dimensions model provides a holistic view of the various constraints, resource types, and other areas that should be considered when designing, managing, or operating an organization. Technology can help organizations to scale up and take on frequent and repetitive tasks, allowing human resources to be used for more complex decision making. However, technology should not always be relied upon without the capability of human intervention, as automation for automation's sake can increase costs and reduce organizational robustness and resilience."

Optimisation means *"to make something as effective and useful as it needs to be. Before an activity can be effectively automated, it should be optimized to whatever degree is possible and reasonable."*

Automation typically refers to *"the use of technology to perform a step or series of steps correctly and consistently with limited or no human intervention"*.

Optimisation activities include:

- Understanding and agreeing the context for optimisation;
- Assessing the current state;
- Agreeing the future state and prioritise, focusing on simplification and value;
- Ensuring stakeholder engagement and commitment;
- Executing improvements iteratively; and
- Monitoring the impact of optimisation continually.

It's important to simplify and/or optimise activities before automation is attempted.

Automation can include:

- Focusing on simplification and optimisation before automation;
- Defining metrics to measure impact and value; and
- Using complementary guiding principles:
  - o Progress iteratively with feedback
  - o Keep it simple and practical
  - o Focus on value
  - o Start where you are

The benefits of automation

Once a task or process has been introduced and performed regularly, often, the next step is to try to automate it. Automation can improve the performance of people, processes, management and organisation structures. It can also improve the way that knowledge and information are shared between parts of the organisation.

Automation can improve the utility and warranty of services, for example:

- Automated resources can have their capacity adjusted more easily;
- Automated resources don't need human intervention, so can be available across time zones or service hours;
- Automated systems can be measured more effectively and improved;
- Computers can optimise services and processes in ways that humans could not; and

- Automation can capture knowledge about a process and share it more easily.

Used carefully, automation can improve service quality and reduce costs and risks. It does this by removing the human element and minimising the chances of a task being performed in different ways by different people.

Automation should reduce complexity and uncertainty. To be automated, a task or process must be clearly defined and understood, or the automation will fail.

Getting ready to automate

Automation will only work if the task or process is broken down into logical steps as part of a workflow that can be programmed into the relevant tool.

There are four main areas to consider when looking at automation:

Table 13: Preparing for Automation

Automation consideration	Details
Simplify the process before automating	Simplification on its own can reduce variation and should not adversely affect the process outcome. However, removal of necessary information or tasks will make the process less useful.
	As a general rule, simplify as far as possible without negative effect, and then automate from this point.

Clarify the process before automation	This will include process activities, tasks and interactions, and inputs. Automate, clarify, test, modify and then automate again, being sure to involve all process agents and stakeholders.
Reduce end-user contact with the underlying systems and processes	We need to try to present our customers with simple options so that they can easily submit demand and extract utility. For example, if a user is requesting a workstation for a new starter, they should not have to answer an endless list of questions about what type of PC they want, how much memory, which supplier it will be ordered from, and so on.
Don't rush to automate complex or non-routine tasks	Automation is of benefit to high volume, low complexity processes. Not everything is suitable for automation, and we may have to accept that some processes are too complex, or not mature enough, to be automated.

Service management automation

Most service management practices will benefit from some level of automation. For example, incident management works well when incident information can be captured and easily transferred between teams. Incident management tools can also automatically notify someone when they are about to breach a target, and something needs to be escalated.

There are many service management tools available, aimed at small, medium and large organisations. Selecting the correct tool can be a real challenge.

When selecting a tool, remember these key points:

- Invest time in requirements gathering, including analysis of your existing toolset; it will pay off.
- Create a long list of available options.
- Carry out a paper review.
- Create a short list and invite suppliers in to demonstrate.
- Select the tool most closely aligned with your budget and requirements.

Every organisation will have different requirements for a service management toolset, but there are some generic considerations, as shown in Table 14.

Table 14: Generic Service Management Toolset Requirements

Generic toolset requirement	Considerations
Self-help	Self-help allows users to access a range of services without speaking directly to someone in the IT department. It is often offered via a web front-end, which needs to connect directly to back-end process handling software.
	Self-help technology integrates these user requests into the back-end process

	management software so that they can be treated in a consistent manner.
	Using technology and automation in this way can mean, for example, that fewer people are required on the service desk answering the phone, and phone calls could be limited to service emergencies and high-priority incidents.
Workflow/ process engine	Automation of workflows and process flows helps ensure that less manual intervention is required when information is passed from team to team, or person to person.
	Responsibilities, mandatory activities and escalation points can also be programmed into a tool with workflow management – so that these are managed automatically too.
Integrated configuration management system (CMS)	An integrated CMS allows information about specific configuration items to be accessed at any time. Configuration items can be linked to incidents, problems, changes and known errors – all via the integrated CMS. (See chapter 11 for more information about configuration management.)
Discovery/ deployment/ licensing	Automated discovery tools dramatically ease the task of updating and changing data in a CMS. Automatically discovering every configuration item on

	the network means only non-networked configuration items will need to be discovered manually and recorded. This removes the danger of people making mistakes during the population of the CMS and allows ongoing verification of the data.
	Any unauthorised changes made to a configuration item will be quickly picked up by the discovery software. This means you can prevent unauthorised items being connected to the network, as well as identifying any configuration items that disappear without approval.
	Discovery technology can also be used to deploy software packages. This helps the organisation to keep track of its software licensing position, as software installs can quickly be compared to the number of licences entered in the CMS.
	An interface to self-help facilities can also be provided via the toolset, to allow request and download of approved software. If this is automatically handled by the deployment software, the service request can be fulfilled with no human intervention, again saving resources.
Remote control	Remote control allows an agent to operate an end user's PC from another location.

	With remote control, the service desk can resolve more incidents at the first point of user contact. Remote-control facilities involve security implications, and these will need to be considered carefully. The organisation might, for example, require a user to click to accept an agent having access to their PC.
Diagnostic utilities	Diagnostic utilities include specially written scripts, routines and programs that are executed to analyse information quickly and provide feedback, typically to help diagnose or record an incident. Within many support organisations, second-line support teams are often critical of the quality of information passed to them by the service desk. Involving these teams in the preparation of diagnostic utilities and scripts means the incident management process can be made more efficient by ensuring that the correct level of information is collected first time. Utilities and scripts will also need to be regularly audited to make sure they are still up to date and fit for purpose.
Reporting	All service management tools should come with some pre-programmed reports that you can leverage quickly, as well as the option to create your own reports – these should be tailored to your

	organisation and the specific targets you have to meet.
	Effective reporting is vital to service management, so any data entered into a toolset should be easy to manipulate and review.
Dashboards	Dashboards provide instant information about service management. For example, a dashboard can allow service level agreement target breaches to be identified quickly and appropriate action taken. Many organisations already use dashboards, often with red-amber-green colours signifying certain conditions.
	Dashboards can be used within IT or made available to customers.

CHAPTER 9: THE SVS: GOVERNANCE

Organisational governance is responsible for evaluating, directing and monitoring an organisation's activities, including its service management.

"Every organization is directed by a governing body, i.e. a person or group of people who are accountable at the highest level for the performance and compliance of the organization. All sizes and types of organization perform governance activities; the governing body may be a board of directors or executive managers how take on a separate governance role when they are performing governance activities. The governing body is accountable for the organization's compliance with policies and any external regulations."

The level of governance within an organisation will be defined by many factors: its size, the industry sector, whether or not it is publicly listed, and the culture within which it operates.

If the governing body doesn't provide clear direction, there is a risk that managers will make decisions that are not aligned with the organisation's overall goals. For example, consider the Volkswagen emissions scandal. Volkswagen Group's vision is "we are a globally leading provider of sustainable mobility", including being a "role model for environment, safety and integrity". Clearly, this vision was not understood by the departments that were creating tests that allowed polluting vehicles onto the road – a decision that ultimately destroyed shareholder value, as well as damaging

Volkswagen's reputation with a broader group of stakeholders.[9]

---

[9] *www.theguardian.com/business/ng-interactive/2015/sep/23/volkswagen-emissions-scandal-explained-diesel-cars.*

CHAPTER 10: THE SVS: THE SERVICE VALUE CHAIN

The service value chain is the central element of the SVS. It is an operating model that outlines the key activities required to respond to demand and facilitate value through products and services. The activities in the value chain are:

- Plan
- Improve
- Engage
- Design and transition
- Obtain/build
- Deliver and support

Figure 9 shows the service value chain[10]:

_____

[10] *ITIL® Foundation, ITIL 4 edition,* figure 4.2.

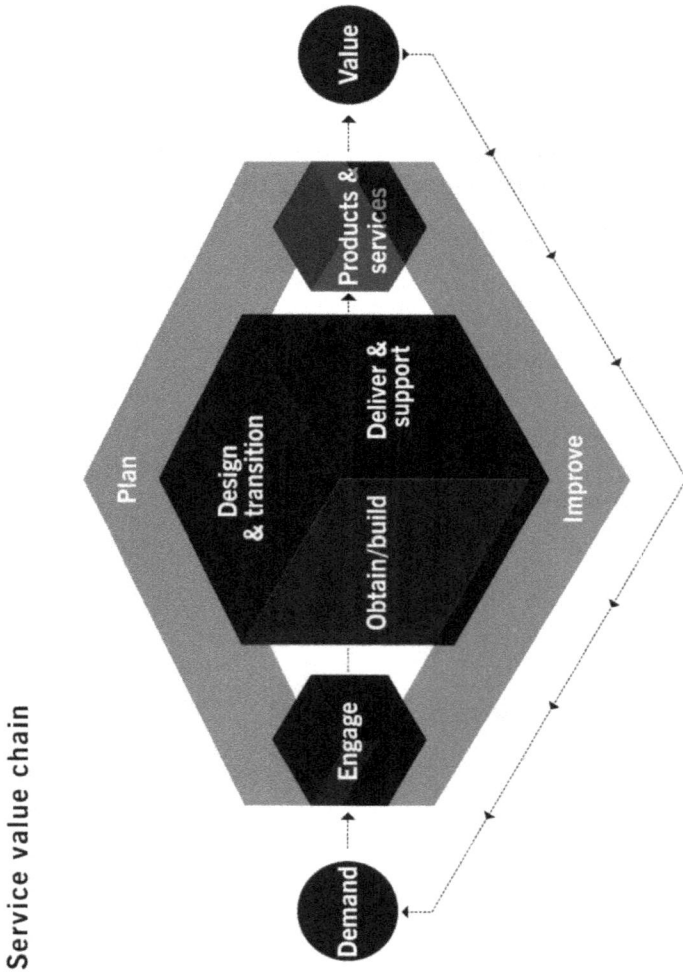

Figure 9: The ITIL service value chain

Activities in the chain don't necessarily happen in a linear flow. Activities may happen in parallel, be repeated, or occur as a series of iterations. Different products, services and consumers will lead to different streams of work and different routes through the value chain. For example, developing a new application will be different from amending an existing one. These are an organisation's value streams: combinations of practices and value chain activities that lead to value.

Each value chain activity relies on inputs and creates outputs for other activities. To convert inputs into outputs, the value chain uses combinations of ITIL practices, which are sets of resources designed for performing certain types of work. Each activity can potentially use:

- Resources
- Processes
- Skills
- Competencies

from one or more ITIL practices, and from inside or outside the organisation.

The activities are all interconnected. Skipping an activity, or spending less time on it than is needed, will impact the whole value chain as other activities will not receive the inputs they need.

There are some key points to remember about the service value chain activities:

- Engage includes **all** engagement interactions – for example, with internal or external customers, suppliers, subject matter experts participating in the organisation's value chain activities, etc. All new resources are obtained through Obtain/build.

- All planning takes place in the Plan activity.
- Component, product and service creation, modification, delivery, maintenance and support are performed in an integrated way by the Design & transition, Obtain/build, and Deliver & support activities.
- Products & services, Demand and Value are SVS components, but they are not value chain activities.

Activity: Plan

"The purpose of the Plan value chain activity is to ensure a shared understanding of the vision, current status, and improvement direction for all four dimensions and all products and services across the organization."

Information inputs into the Plan activity are used to create key outputs including improvement opportunities (for Improve) and contract agreements (for Engage).

Table 15: Key Inputs and Outputs of the Plan Activity

Key inputs to the *Plan activity*	• Policies, requirements and constraints; • Consolidated demand and opportunities (from *Engage*); • Value chain performance information, improvement initiatives and plans (from *Improve*); • Improvement status reports (from *Improve*);

	<ul><li>Knowledge and information about new or changed products and services (from *Design & transition* and *Obtain/build*); and</li><li>Knowledge and information about externally provided service components (from *Engage*).</li></ul>
Key outputs from the *Plan activity*	<ul><li>Strategic, tactical and operational plans;</li><li>Portfolio decisions for *Design & transition*;</li><li>Architectures and policies;</li><li>Improvement opportunities (for *Improve*);</li><li>Contract and agreement requirements (for *Engage*); and</li><li>Product and service portfolio (for *Engage*).</li></ul>

Activity: Improve

"The purpose of the Improve value chain activity is to ensure continual improvement of products, services and practices across all value chain activities and the four dimensions of service management."

Deliver & support provides service performance information and Engage provides stakeholder feedback. Outputs include improvement initiatives, status reports and service performance information for Design & transition.

🌐 **Table 16: Key Inputs and Outputs of the Improve Activity**

Key inputs to the *Improve activity*	• Product and service performance information (from *Deliver & support*); • Stakeholder feedback (from *Engage*); • Performance information and improvement opportunities (from all value chain activities); • Knowledge and information about new or changed products and services (from *Design & transition* and *Obtain/build*); and • Knowledge and information about externally provided service components (from *Engage*).
Key outputs from the *Improve activity*	• Improvement initiatives and plans (for all value chain activities, products and services); • Value chain performance information (for *Plan*, and the governing body); • Improvement status reports (for all value chain activities); • Contract and agreement requirements (for *Engage*); and • Service performance information (for *Design & transition*).

Activity: Engage

📋 *"The purpose of the Engage value chain activity is to provide a good understanding of stakeholder needs, transparency, and continual engagement and good relationships with all stakeholders."*

Engage provides oversight of requests and feedback from customers, as well as incidents to help identify Improve opportunities. Engage is not only about engagement with customers but also with suppliers, subject matter experts in the business, management and all stakeholders.

🌐 **Table 17: Key Inputs and Outputs of the Engage Activity**

Key inputs to the *Engage activity*	• The product and service portfolio (from *Plan*); • Demand and opportunities for products and services (from internal and external customers); • Detailed requirements, requests and feedback (from internal and external customers); • Incidents, service requests and feedback (from users); • Information on the completion of user support tasks (from *Deliver & support*); • Marketing opportunities (from current and potential customers and users);

	<ul><li>Cooperation opportunities and feedback (from partners and suppliers);</li><li>Contract and agreement requirements (from all value chain activities);</li><li>Knowledge and information about new or changed products and services (from *Design & transition* and *Obtain/build*);</li><li>Knowledge and information about externally provided service components (from partners and suppliers); and</li><li>Improvement initiatives and improvement status reports (from *Improve*).</li></ul>
Key outputs from the *Engage* activity	<ul><li>Consolidated demands and opportunities (for *Plan*);</li><li>Product and service requirements (for *Design & transition*);</li><li>User support tasks (for *Deliver & support*);</li><li>Improvement opportunities and stakeholder feedback (for *Improve*);</li><li>Change or project initiation requests (for *Obtain/build*); and</li><li>Contracts and agreements with external and internal suppliers and</li></ul>

	partied (for *Design & transition* and *Obtain/build*).

Activity: Design & transition

"The purpose of the Design and Transition value chain activity is to ensure that products and services continually meet stakeholder expectations for quality, costs and time to market."

This activity receives portfolio decisions as an input, as well as information about components provided by suppliers from Engage. This activity will create (among other outputs) requirements and specifications that are passed to Obtain/build and contract requirements that are passed to Engage.

Table 18: Key Inputs and Outputs of the Design and Transition Activity

Key inputs to the *Design & transition* activity	• Portfolio decisions, architectures and policies (from *Plan*); • Product and service requirements (from *Engage*); • Improvement initiatives and improvement status reports (from *Improve*); • Service performance information (from *Deliver & support*, and *Improve*); • Service components (from *Obtain/build*);

	• Knowledge and information about externally provided service components (from *Engage*); and • Knowledge and information about new or changed products and services (from *Obtain/build*).
Key outputs from the *Design & transition activity*	• Requirements and specifications (for *Obtain/build*); • Contract and agreement requirements (for *Engage*); • New and changed products and services (from *Deliver & support*); • Knowledge and information about new or changed services (for all value chain activities); and • Performance information and improvement opportunities (for *Improve*).

Activity: Obtain/build

"The purpose of the Obtain/Build value chain activity is to ensure that service components are available when and where they are needed and meet agreed specifications."

Organisations need to decide whether to create products and services themselves, or to use external resources, or a combination.

🌐 **Table 19: Key Inputs and Outputs of the Obtain/Build Activity**

Key inputs to the *Obtain/build activity*	• Architecture and policies (from *Plan*); • Contracts and agreements (from *Engage*); • Goods and services (from internal and external suppliers and partners); • Requirements and specifications (from *Design & transition*); • Improvement initiatives and status reports (from *Improve*); • Change or project initiation requests (from *Engage*); • Change requests (from *Deliver & support*); • Knowledge and information about new or changed products and services (from *Design & transition*); and • Knowledge and information about externally provided service components (from *Engage*).
Key outputs from the *Obtain/build activity*	• Service components (for *Deliver & support* and *Design & transition*); • Knowledge and information about new or changed service components (for all value chain activities); • Contract and agreement requirements (for *Engage*); and

	• Performance information and improvement opportunities (for *Improve*).

Activity: Deliver & support

📋 *"The purpose of the Deliver and Support value chain activity is to ensure that services are delivered and supported according to agreed specifications and stakeholders' expectations."*

This activity will receive new or updated services, including service components from Obtain/build and user support tasks from Improve. The outputs will include the new or updated service being offered to users.

🌐 **Table 20: Key Inputs and Outputs of the Deliver and Support Activity**

Key inputs to the *Deliver & support activity*	• New or changed products and services (from *Design & transition*); • Contracts and agreements (from *Engage*); • Service components (from *Obtain/build*); • Improvement initiatives and status reports (from *Improve*); • User support tasks (from *Engage*); • Knowledge and information about new or changed products and services and components (from *Design & transition* and *Obtain/build*); and

	• Knowledge and information about externally provided service components (from *Engage*).
Key outputs from the *Deliver & support activity*	• Services (delivered to customers and users); • Information on the completion of user support tasks (for *Engage*); • Product and service performance information (for *Engage and Improve);* • Improvement opportunities (for *Improve*); • Contract and agreement requirements (for *Engage*); • Change requests (for *Obtain/build*); and • Service performance information (for *Design & transition*).

CHAPTER 11: ITIL PRACTICES INTRODUCED

"A practice is a set of organizational resources designed for performing work or accomplishing an objective."

Each ITIL practice supports multiple service value chain activities. Practices are made up by resources from the four dimensions of service management:

- Organizations and people
- Information and technology
- Partners and suppliers
- Value streams and processes

The ITIL SVS features 34 practices:

- 14 general management practices
- 17 service management practices
- 3 technical management practices

Table 21: ITIL Practice Types

General management practice	These practices are adopted and adapted for service management from business management.
Service management practice	These practices have originated and developed in service management and ITSM.
Technical management practice	These practices originated in technology management and have

	been adapted for service management.

In the following chapters we will look at the 34 practices in more detail, including practice considerations based on the author's experiences working in ITSM. Remember that these practices are part of the ITIL SVS.

From processes to practices

One of the notable changes that has taken place in the evolution from ITIL v3 to ITIL 4 is a shift in terminology from 'processes' to 'practices'.

The ITIL definition of a practice is:

"A set of organizational resources designed for performing work or accomplishing an objective."

The ITIL definition of a process is:

"A set of interrelated or interacting activities that transform inputs into outputs. A process takes one or more defined inputs and turns them into defined outputs. Processes define the sequence of actions and their dependencies."

This change will have an impact on many ITSM organisations that are used to thinking in terms of processes (for example, an incident management process), and assigning roles, creating procedures, etc. within a process framework. The change from processes to practices is partly driven by a need to address a criticism often levelled at ITIL – that it is bureaucratic, inflexible and doesn't integrate with newer ways of working like Agile and DevOps that are gaining popularity in IT. ITIL 4 encourages organisations to think beyond process workflows and, for each practice area, to consider:

- People and teams
- Suppliers and partner relationships
- Roles, skills and competencies
- Continual improvement
- Information and data
- Supporting technology and toolsets
- Metrics, measurement and reporting
- Interfaces

Processes, procedures and policies still have relevance but are now part of a wider practice-based perspective.

What does this mean for organisations that have an established, process-driven approach for ITSM? As with any organisational change, it certainly doesn't mean creating massive upheaval for no reason. ITSM teams can analyse whether their processes are effective and look at the broader practice perspective as part of their regular process improvement analysis activities. Look for opportunities to make an improvement, but don't make changes for the sake of it.

The common sense, good practices for ITSM processes are still relevant; here's a reminder. Processes should be:

- Closed-loop systems
- Documents and shared
- Directed by policies
- Reusable

To be effective, service management processes should be set up as closed-loop systems. This means that they should request feedback and use it to improve the way they perform.

If processes don't work on this closed-loop model, they will not improve, and no lessons will be learned. From an ITIL 4 perspective, the process feedback is used holistically to make improvements across the SVS; processes do not operate in isolation.

Processes should also be documented so they can be shared and used throughout an organisation. If there isn't a definitive agreed version of a process, different teams will carry out the activities in different ways – all of them believing they are following the process properly.

Processes are directed by policies. Policies are used to document management expectations and their intentions for the process. The policy is then used to make sure the process development and implementation is done in a way that is consistent with management intentions. From an ITIL 4 perspective, policies will be driven by governance and principles defined as part of the SVS.

Within service management, one of the ways that processes deliver value is by being reusable. This means, for example, that one change enablement process can be used across the organisation, rather than each programme or project developing its own change enablement process. Reusable processes can be measured, monitored and improved.

Process models

To support organisational understanding of processes, we can document them using a process model. A process model is a way of designing and mapping a process and can be effective if you need to develop a new process or update an existing one. Figure 10 shows a simplified process model.

Every process must have inputs and outputs. An input triggers a process, for example, a call to a service desk will start the fault resolution or diagnostic process.

Outputs mean the iteration of the process is complete and it has served its purpose. As part of the output, the process requests feedback, which makes sure it is working as a closed loop – learning lessons about how it is working and its level of customer satisfaction.

Activities that need to happen to turn the input into an output are documented in the 'activities' box. These activities might include roles, procedures, workflows and metrics.

Process controls should also be in place to make sure the process works properly and doesn't become ineffective over time. Controls could include nominating a process owner, checking the process' alignment with policy and principles, and checking the feedback received.

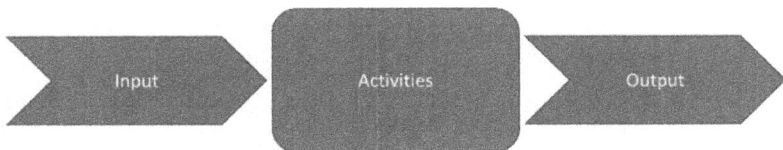

Figure 10: A simple process model

Process enablers is a term used to describe the resources that we use to make the process work, for example, technology or people. A perfect process will deliver no value if there aren't enough resources to implement it.

Remember: a process model doesn't have to be complicated. You can start by brainstorming the process with a group of stakeholders. This will help you document the right steps, so that they can be agreed. Once a common process is defined and agreed, you can automate it using a service management toolset, if appropriate. Process models are also useful for education, as they are a quick and easy way to explain a process to staff members. You will notice that this is similar to the value stream mapping exercise we described in earlier chapters. Both process modelling and value stream mapping are useful ways to make work visible, helping to get consensus from stakeholders and identify issues and bottlenecks.

Have a go: why not draw your own process model? Incident management and change enablement are great places to start.

CHAPTER 12: GENERAL MANAGEMENT PRACTICES

In today's climate of digital transformation, the lines between what is an 'IT' practice or process and what is a 'business' practice or process are blurred. All areas of the organisation must work together for it to be able to deliver the services its customers want, at an appropriate level of quality and at the right speed. For example, some organisations that have adopted Agile software development methods now find that they are struggling to deliver value because their procurement or budgetary practices do not align with an iterative and incremental way of working.

As part of this transformation, IT ways of working are also extending into business departments (often referred to as enterprise service management (ESM)) and IT is adopting good practices from the business. An example of this is the widespread adoption of Agile ways of working outside of software development teams, and the use of service management tools to track and update personnel information.

The ITIL general management practices are examples of domains that have both an IT and a wider business relevance. For example, supplier management has relevance for both IT and non-IT suppliers. Where the IT department has developed effective ways of working, these should be shared with the rest of the organisation. Where the rest of the organisation has developed effective ways of working, IT teams should seek to adopt them.

12: General management practices

Continual improvement

The ITIL 4 Foundation syllabus requires in-depth study of continual improvement; other practices only require familiarity with the practice purpose and some key definitions. Some practices are entirely excluded from the ITIL Foundation syllabus. Watch out for the symbols in each practice section if you're preparing for your ITIL 4 Foundation exam.

📋 Denotes syllabus-related content.

📋 *"The purpose of the continual improvement practice is to align the organization's practices and services with changing business needs through the ongoing improvement of products, services and practices, or any element involved in the management of products and services."*

Continual improvement records improvement opportunities in the continual improvement register (CIR). This can be a written document, spreadsheet or database. It allows improvement ideas to be logged, prioritised, tracked and managed. Some ideas are never implemented because of cost or timing issues. Each idea is:

- Documented
- Assessed
- Prioritised
- Implemented if appropriate
- Reviewed

Continual improvement needs to happen at all levels of the organisation:

- Leaders must embed continual improvement and create a culture that allows it to thrive.
- The continual improvement practice will be accountable for continual improvement and will promote it across the organisation.
- All staff will participate in continual improvement; it must be seen as part of everyone's role.
- Suppliers and partners should also contribute to improvement initiatives; this is often included in their contracts, which describe how improvements are reported and measured.

Continual improvement activities include:

- Encouraging continual improvement across the organisation;
- Securing time and budget for continual improvement;
- Identifying and logging improvement opportunities;
- Assessing and prioritising improvement opportunities;
- Making business cases for improvement action;
- Planning and implementing improvements;
- Measuring and evaluating improvement results; and
- Coordinating improvement activities across the organisation.

There are many different methods and techniques that continual improvement can use. It's important to select the right technique for the right situation, rather than trying to use them all at once. Methods and techniques include:

- Lean
- Multi-phase project
- Maturity assessments
- DevOps
- Balanced scorecard
- Incremental or Agile improvements
- Quick wins
- SWOT analysis (strengths, weaknesses, opportunities and threats)

The continual improvement model

Figure 11 shows the continual improvement model:

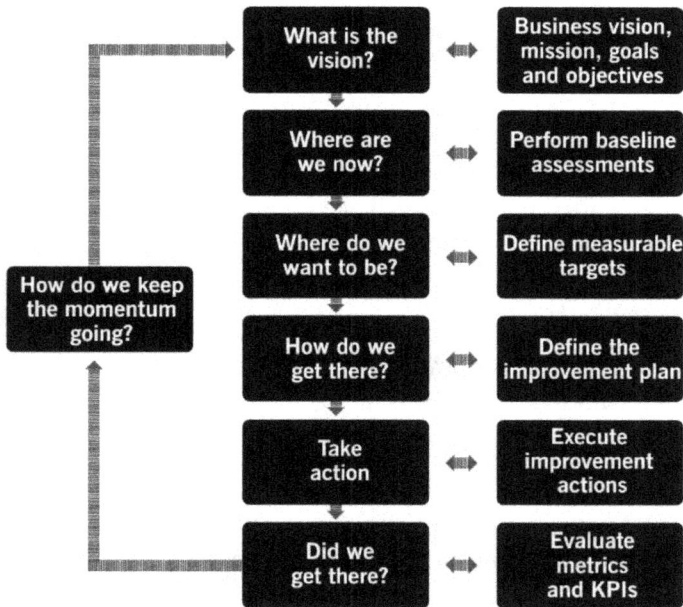

Figure 11: The continual improvement model[11]

The continual improvement model provides a high-level guide for improvement initiatives. It allows organisations to focus on customer value and link back to their vision. Following the steps in the model allows work to be divided into manageable sections, so small goals are achieved and momentum is maintained. Improvement is not a one-off

---

[11] *ITIL® Foundation, ITIL 4 edition*, figure 4.3.

activity – as one improvement initiative completes, another begins.

Practice considerations

What needs to be fixed or improved in an organisation can be a very subjective matter. Everyone will have a different opinion about what's wrong and what needs to be fixed first, based on the services they use and their own experience and world view.

Service provider organisations are as blameworthy as customers and users in this area. They make assumptions about what needs to be fixed and what's important to their consumers, without having all the information they need.

Following an approach like the continual improvement model provides structure for improvement activities. The first time you follow the model, it can feel laborious, manual and frustrating, but it should get you to the desired result. The next time you follow the model, it will be a bit easier, and it will get easier and easier with each iteration. Eventually, this iterative approach to improvement will become part of your culture and normal ways of working.

There are few feelings worse than standing in front of senior management presenting something based on inaccurate or incomplete data. Use the model to make sure your data stacks up, and test your findings on your peers before you take them to the management team.

Putting continual improvement to work

To make continual improvement work in your organisation, here are some important points to consider.

Continual improvement includes cultural change: the primary mistake made when implementing continual improvement is to allocate staff to roles and think 'job done'. Continual improvement needs to run through every activity and every role in the organisation. If continual improvement is seen as a team rather than an organisation-wide practice, the team will quickly become a dumping ground for everything hard and problematic.

Continual improvement does not just apply to live services: improvements made during development can be extremely effective. For example, it is widely accepted that making corrections to a service during design is much more cost-effective than fixing a service that has gone live. Continual improvement also applies to all four dimensions of service management, not just to services themselves.

Don't jump to conclusions: many organisations start by implementing something that they think will lead to improvements. They don't carefully assess what is wrong or what needs to be done, because they assume that they already know. This is dangerous and can lead to resources being wasted and IT appearing arrogant.

Effective continual improvement relies on a balanced set of measurements: service provider organisations need to measure the emotional, intangible indicators (for example, customers who 'just aren't happy') and the tangible facts (for example, 'time to complete a transaction'). Both areas are required to get a holistic view of overall service performance.

But... don't get carried away with the measurements: modern technology allows us to measure every element of a service, producing far more data that we are equipped to handle. Focus on a few, meaningful measurements and expand from there, if you need to. The more mature the service management organisation, the less it tends to measure.

🌐 Architecture management

"The purpose of the architecture management practice is to provide an understanding of all the different elements that make up an organization and how those elements interrelate, enabling the organization to effectively achieve its current and future objectives. It provides the principles, standards and tools that enable an organization to manage complex change in a structured and Agile way."

Architecture management provides visibility and coordination. As Peter Drucker famously said, "you can't manage what you can't measure." We could add: you can't measure what you can't visualise. Architecture management as a practice addresses multiple domains:

- Business
- Service
- Information
- Technology
- Environment

The architecture types are:

- **Business architecture:** allows the organisation's capabilities to be compared with its strategy to identify gaps.
- **Service architecture:** provides a view of all services and interactions between services.
- **Information systems architecture:** provides a view of the logical and physical data and information assets of

the organisation, including how they are managed and shared.

- **Technology architecture:** defines the software and hardware infrastructure of the organisation.
- **Environmental architecture:** describes external factors affecting the organisation, and environmental controls. This could include a PESTEL analysis.

Practice considerations

Enterprise architecture is often viewed as a complex practice and, in some organisations, is seen as having a purely technical focus. From an ITIL 4 perspective, effective architecture management is essential, as it will underpin many of the decisions made and the activities carried out within the SVS.

When new services are being developed or existing services are being changed, architecture management can help to provide 'blueprint' information to support effective decision making. Architecture management input into portfolio decisions can include:

- Architectural directives/policies;
- Advice on existing architecture, and any opportunities and limitations; and
- Information about the impact of changes and possible dependencies.

A good first step with architecture management is to identify what information already exists and where (and, of course, whether it's up to date!). There may already be defined architecture roles and information that you can access. Next, make sure architecture management is integrated with decision-making processes and is able to provide input at appropriate times. Many benefits can be realised from effective architecture management; for example, having a clear technology roadmap prevents money and time being wasted on inappropriate technical initiatives.

Information security management

"The purpose of the information security management practice is to protect the information needed by the organization to conduct its business. This includes understanding and managing risks to the confidentiality, integrity and availability of information, as well as other aspects of information security such as authentication (ensuring someone is who they claim to be) and non-repudiation (ensuring that someone can't deny that they took an action)."

An effective information security practice will include:

- Policies
- Processes
- Behaviours
- Risk management
- Controls

The controls established by an organisation need to balance:

- **Prevention** – making sure that security incidents don't occur.
- **Detection** – detecting incidents that couldn't be prevented quickly and reliably.

- **Correction** – recovering from incidents.

The information security management practice must balance protecting the organisation with a pragmatic approach to keeping it secure. If the controls in place are seen as restrictive, staff will actively avoid them, creating a greater risk than might perhaps be posed by slightly looser controls.

Information security management is a practice that spans the entire organisation. Technological controls can be used (for example, two-factor authentication), but people and their behaviour are the most essential area of focus. Many security breaches are behaviour related, and social engineering is often used in security testing and planning exercises. For example, tests might include asking staff to let someone into a building without a key card, because they've forgotten a vital document.

Practice considerations

Many service management practices and processes are implemented in silos, and information security management is often no exception. It's common for someone to be put 'in charge' of security and then left to get on with it. Without management support, they may feel like they are being given an impossible task, trying to get other staff to follow the policies and procedures they are implementing.

Management backing is essential for this process. Staff may be resistant to changing their behaviour. It can be hard to achieve cultural change with a bottom-up implementation – top-down direction and support from management is needed. Identifying any relevant legislation and regulations that affect your organisation can be helpful to make the case for information security management; clearly communicate why information is important, along with the consequences of a possible breach.

Considering security at the design stage can be extremely helpful. If a service goes live with security measures built in, there will be less manual work to do later.

A lot of information security management is automated. Access management for services, audit trails, etc. all support effective information security management. We should not, however, rely on automation alone to implement information security management – the biggest danger to any organisation is usually the person sitting at the desk.

Knowledge management

"The purpose of the knowledge management practice is to maintain and improve the effective, efficient and convenient use of information and knowledge across the organization."

Knowledge is an intangible asset for an organisation. The knowledge management practice will provide a structured approach to:

- Defining knowledge
- Building knowledge (including capturing knowledge)
- Reusing knowledge
- Sharing knowledge

Many factors affect the knowledge management practice, including the size and complexity of the organisation. Knowledge management might include paper records and spreadsheets, or complex automated solutions with functionality including search, natural language processing and the ability to 'rate' articles.

12: General management practices

Knowledge is information presented in context. An effective knowledge management practice ensures that the right person receives the right information, in the right format, at the right level and at the right time.

🌐 Practice considerations

Think about your own organisation. If you need to find out how to carry out a task, how much work does that involve? Is knowledge easily accessible? Do you have to ask people, or is it stored in a system or spreadsheet? Consider how much time you and your team spend rediscovering knowledge.

Knowledge management is one of the most nebulous areas of service management. Knowledge exists in so many forms and so many places in an organisation – the idea of bringing it all under control can be difficult to imagine.

Organisations need to think creatively when it comes to knowledge management. How are staff sharing knowledge right now? They might be using systems or services that have previously been thought of as personal, such as social media.

It's common to find cultural barriers hampering your knowledge management implementation. Some staff members like to hold on to knowledge to make themselves feel valuable, safe and needed. The knowledge management strategy will have to address incentives for staff to share knowledge – it could even be included as part of individual objectives.

Too much knowledge is as damaging as too little. You might have experience of situations where knowledge bases are put in place that quickly fill up with duplicated, incorrect or irrelevant information. Proper knowledge management will prevent the organisation being overwhelmed by content.

Analysing the cost of poor knowledge management can be a good way to build a business case for improvements. For example, many consultancy organisations with which I've worked have had poor knowledge management. Each engagement is treated as a new project, with knowledge assets being recreated from scratch. This all consumes billable hours. Creating standard, reusable assets to support consultancy engagements should be a simple idea to sell, but again, you might find politics and knowledge hoarding get in your way.

Measurement and reporting

"The purpose of the measurement and reporting practice is to support good decision-making by decreasing the levels of uncertainty. This is achieved through the collection of relevant data on various managed objects and the valid assessment of this data in an appropriate context. Managed objects include, but are not limited to, products and services, practices and value chain activities, suppliers and partners, and the organization as a whole."

Most organisations manage a range of metrics from high-level organisational objectives to lower-level, operational and component metrics. Organisational goals and legislative and regulatory requirements will drive the metrics that are implemented, including:

- Profit
- Growth
- Competitive advantage
- Customer retention
- Compliance (with legislation and regulations)

Critical success factors (CSFs) and key performance indicators (KPIs) can be agreed and implemented to help assess performance against these organisational goals.

A CSF is *"a necessary precondition for the achievement of intended results"*. A KPI is *"an important metric used to evaluate the success in meeting an objective"*.

Goodhart's law applies to measurement and reporting: "When a measure becomes a target, it ceases to be a good measure."

Organisations need to continually review the metrics they have in place to make sure they are not driving poor behaviours or creating unintended effects. Linking KPIs to organisational goals and value – and applying KPIs to teams rather than the individual – can help reduce any negative impact.

Most organisations present the data they collect in reports or dashboards. Data should be presented with a purpose in mind: to inform, or to support decision making or prioritisation.

Practice considerations

Measurement and reporting has undergone significant change in the past 5–10 years. Looking back, many organisations were stuck in a monthly reporting cycle, with staff members spending hours producing reports, often including printing and binding them only to find they were glanced at or ignored in management meetings.

Now, reporting tends to be just in time and at a glance. A report that tells you what happened last week will feel out of date, let alone one that looks back over four weeks. Managers and team members want to be able to see what is happening now, and understand how trends are building up over time.

Spend some time assessing the reporting in your organisation:

- Are reports shared widely or only circulated to a few people?
- Is unnecessary manual reporting taking place?
- Are reports being used?
- What ad hoc reports are requested?

Using reporting and dashboards to make performance visible can help ensure everyone is 'on the same page'; this encourages communication and collaboration between teams.

Finally, reflect on this quote from E.M. Goldratt (author of *The Goal*): "Tell me how you measure me, and I will tell you how I will behave."

Organisational change management

"The purpose of the organizational change management practice is to ensure that changes in an organization are smoothly and successfully implemented, and that lasting benefits are achieved by managing the human aspects of the changes."

Change in an organisation will affect people, including:

- How they work
- How they behave

- Their role

Organisational change management (OCM) works to:

- Gain acceptance and support for changes;
- Remove or reduce resistance to change;
- Eliminate or address adverse change impacts;
- Provide training and awareness; and
- Carry out any other activities to support a successful transition.

OCM will be active throughout the whole of the SVS, whenever change is affecting people. OCM will establish and maintain:

- Clear and relevant objectives for the change
- Strong and committed leadership
- Wiling and prepared participants
- Sustained improvement

OCM activities include:

- Creating a sense of urgency
- Stakeholder management
- Sponsor management
- Communication
- Empowerment
- Resistance management
- Reinforcement

Accountability for OCM should not be transferred to an external supplier; someone within the organisation should remain accountable. External experts may be used to support OCM if the skills don't exist within the organisation.

Practice considerations

There are many tools and techniques that you can use to support change management efforts.

Kotter's eight-step model is popular:

1. Create a sense of urgency
2. Build a guiding coalition
3. Form a strategic vision and initiatives
4. Enlist a volunteer army
5. Enable action by removing barriers
6. Generate short-term wins
7. Sustain acceleration
8. Institute change

Lewin's change management model is also frequently used:

- Unfreeze the organisation
- Change
- Refreeze the organisation

OCM thinking is also evolving in the world of digital transformation, and many practitioners are focused on treating OCM as an ongoing state of permanent change, rather than a series of projects. To quote change expert Karen Ferris: "Change is the new black! To survive in today's reality, adaptive leadership and relentless evolution are vital."

However, as Antoine de Saint-Exupéry said: "A goal without a plan is just a wish." All the change techniques in the world won't help unless you can take people along with you. Consider previous changes in your organisation and whether they have been successful or not. Look at your culture, your structure and how long employees have remained with the organisation. To quote the ITIL principle, "start where you are. Plan for reality and be prepared for possible resistance."

Portfolio management

"The purpose of the portfolio management practice is to ensure that the organization has the right mix of programmes, projects, products and services to execute the organization's strategy within its funding and resource constraints."

Portfolio management includes making the strategic decisions that balance organisational change and business as usual. The practice activities include:

- Developing and applying a framework to define and deliver the portfolio of products, services, programmes and projects to support strategies and objectives;
- Defining products and services and linking them to agreed outcomes;
- Evaluating and prioritising product, service, project and change proposals;
- Implementing a strategic investment appraisal and decision-making process for portfolio decisions;
- Analysing and tracking investments to identify value;
- Monitoring the performance of the portfolio and adjusting it to meet organisational priority changes; and
- Reviewing portfolios to assess progress, outcomes, costs, risk, benefits and strategic contribution.

The scope of portfolio management includes:

- **Product/service portfolio** – the complete set of products and services managed by an organisation, both new and planned.
- **Project portfolio** – provides a view of all authorised projects.
- **Customer portfolio** – maintained by the relationship management practices, recording the organisation's customers.

Practice considerations

Portfolio management relies on accurate information to be successful. If new services are commissioned and the portfolio management is not informed, the service portfolio will be out of date very quickly. The practice needs ongoing resources and care after it is established.

It is important to make sure the practice is involved in the full lifecycle of products and services all the way through to retirement. It's dangerous to focus solely on new services. Many organisations continue to spend money and time on old services that don't deliver value and could be retired.

Portfolio management needs to have a clear understanding of strategic objectives. A service that delivers value is a service that meets business objectives. Service value can only be assessed if portfolio management actually understands the business objectives. A poor relationship with the business will be very damaging for this practice.

🌐 Project management

"The purpose of the project management practice is to ensure that all projects in the organization are successfully delivered. This is achieved by planning, delegating, monitoring, and maintaining control of all aspects of a project, and keeping the motivation of the people involved."

A project is *"a temporary structure that is created for the purpose of delivering one or more outputs (or products) according to an agreed business case"*.

Projects can be used as a vehicle to deliver a significant change to an organisation. They might be standalone, or part of a larger programme or portfolio of changes.

Projects may be delivered using an Agile or a waterfall approach:

- **Waterfall** – works well when requirements are known upfront, and where the definition of work is more valuable than the speed of delivery.
- **Agile** – works well when requirements are uncertain or likely to evolve, and where speed of delivery is prioritised over the definition of precise requirements.

Project management can help organisations balance:

- Maintaining current business operations;
- Transforming business operations as the market changes; and
- Continually improving products and services.

12: General management practices

🌐 Practice considerations

Traditional project management practices are well documented in the PRINCE2® publications issued by AXELOS. The Project Management Institute (PMI) also offers guidance and support for project managers. Agile project management practices are documented in *PRINCE2 Agile* (published by AXELOS) and *Agile Project Management* (published by the Agile Business Consortium).

In my experience, the main reasons that projects fail are:

- Unclear objectives/deliverables
- Lack of resources
- Unmanaged changes to project scope or deadlines (for example, scope creep)

These risk factors will apply to both an Agile and a waterfall environment. The role of the project manager is still essential, and a good project manager can help a project to be successful by maintaining a focus on expectation setting and good communication.

In some organisations, employees feel torn between their business-as-usual (BAU) work and project work. If this is the case for you, seek clarity from your line manager about where your time is best spent.

Relationship management

📋 *"The purpose of the relationship management practice is to establish and nurture the links between the organization and its stakeholders at strategic and tactical levels. It includes the identification, analysis, monitoring and continual improvement of relationships with and between stakeholders."*

The relationship management practice will ensure that:

- Stakeholders' needs and motivations are understood, allowing effective prioritisation;
- Stakeholder satisfaction is high and there is a constructive relationship between the organisation and stakeholders;
- Customer priorities are established and articulated, in alignment with business outcomes;
- Products and services facilitate value creation for service consumers and the organisation;
- The organisation is facilitating value for all stakeholders; and
- Conflicting stakeholder requirements are identified and mediated.

Relationship management needs to include all relevant stakeholders. Many organisations focus on consumers and customers, but suppliers, partners, employees, etc. are all significant.

Practice considerations

Relationship management is often implemented as a quick fix when customer satisfaction is low. To be effective, the practice needs to be involved throughout the SVS. The practice should be proactive and involved early on, not brought in at the end when things go wrong.

If a service provider organisation has a poor relationship with its customers, relationship management might struggle to improve the situation immediately. Patience is required – things will only improve when the customer trusts the service provider organisation and shares information.

Relationship management will only be effective if it is seen as a neutral area. If the customer believes the practice always favours the service provider organisation, or vice versa, it will not be effective. Relationship management staff need to be ethical and responsible. Sometimes they will have to deliver tough messages, but it's better to tell a hard truth than to mislead either party.

For many organisations, relationship problems develop because the customer can't explain what they want in IT terms and regard the IT staff as speaking 'techie speak'. Relationship management can provide a useful translation service.

Applying relationship management to supplier and partner relationships is growing in importance. Once the contract is signed, relationship management can be applied to situations where things need to be slightly different. A good relationship leads to 'give and take' on both sides that can avoid costly and lengthy contractual renegotiations.

If you're interested in relationship management, take a look at the Business Relationship Management Institute website:

https://brm.institute.

For partner and supplier management, read more about service integration and management and the role of the service integrator, starting with the SIAM Body of Knowledge information at:

www.scopism.com.

🌐 Risk management

"The purpose of the risk management practice is to ensure that the organization understands and handles risks effectively. Managing risk is essential to ensuring the ongoing sustainability of an organization and creating value for its customers. Risk management is an integral part of all organizational activities and therefore central to an organization's SVS."

Risk is often viewed as something negative, but it is also associated with opportunity. Failing to take an opportunity (or being unprepared for it) can also be a risk, which needs to be avoided.

Risk management will create a portfolio of risks, which map to the project, product, customer and service portfolio. Effective service management creates products and services that are opportunities to identify and capture value, rather than risks associated with unfulfilled demand. Risk management needs to balance the cost of addressing a risk against the potential impact of the risk. This will be partly dictated by the organisation's strategy and culture; an innovative organisation will be more willing to accept the risk of failure if it leads to new products and services.

Effective risk management will:

- Identify risks
- Assess risks
- Treat risks in an appropriate manner

There are some principles that apply specifically to risk management:

- Risk is part of the business – not all risks can or need to be avoided.
- Risk management must be consistent across the organisation.
- Risk management culture and behaviours are important.

Further information on risk management can be found in ISO 31000:2018, which states that the 'purpose of risk management is the creation and protection of value'.

Practice considerations

As with most of the ITIL practices, there is a strong 'people' element in risk management:

- If leaders don't treat risk management as important, the rest of the organisation won't see it as a priority.
- If managers are punished for delivering bad news, they will be reluctant to report risks.
- If staff don't understand the organisation's risk appetite, they may take unnecessary risks during their work.

Creating a risk log can be a useful exercise to try to understand how the organisation perceives risk and its level of tolerance. You could try this exercise with your team, or with a group of stakeholders with a common interest:

- Describe each risk and its potential impact.
- Allocate a probability score.
- Allocate an impact score.

- This will give a risk score based on the 'impact x probability' scores.
- Describe a possible mitigation plan.
- Re-score the risk if the mitigation plan was already in place.

This exercise might raise some risks that surprise you! It is a useful way to see which risks need to be addressed as a priority, and to identify if there are any quick wins you can implement to mitigate them. Make sure each risk also has a unique number, a date when it was raised, an owner and a status.

Service financial management

"The purpose of the service financial management practice is to support the organization's strategies and plans for service management by ensuring that the organization's financial resources and investments are being used effectively."

Service financial management supports decision making by the organisation's governing body and management. The practice is responsible for budgeting, costing, accounting and charging activities:

- Budgeting/costing: focuses on predicting and controlling income and expenditure within the organisation.
- Accounting: accounts for how money is being spent.
- Charging: invoices service consumers (where relevant).

🌐 Practice considerations

Some organisations believe that their overall organisational financial management process is sufficient, and do not invest in service financial management. In my experience, this is a mistake. Service financial management will break down the cost of IT services in more detail than the organisational financial management process, which will lead to better IT investment decisions in the future.

Service financial management can be complicated to implement. General IT staff will not usually have the skills required, so they will need training or support from staff with financial qualifications and experience.

Many organisations are constantly trying to reduce the cost of providing IT services. Service financial management should focus on cost optimisation rather than cost cutting. Cost optimisation looks at the most efficient way to provide the services required by the business, not cutting a set percentage off the IT spend year on year. Costs can only be cut so far before service quality suffers.

Organisations that have adopted Agile ways of working may find their development practices and their financial practices are in conflict. For example, an Agile project might start with a minimum set of requirements and enough information for the first sprint; this won't help in an organisation that demands detailed business cases and 12-month plans to sign off any expenditure. It's important to make sure that any conflict between practices is identified and addressed.

12: General management practices

Strategy management

🌐 *"The purpose of the strategy management practice is to formulate the goals of the organization and adopt the courses of action and allocation of resources necessary for achieving those goals. Strategy management establishes the organization's direction, focuses effort, defines or clarifies the organization's priorities, and provides consistency or guidance in response to the environment."*

An organisation's strategy defines desired outcomes, so that resources, capabilities and investments can be prioritised to deliver them. The practice ensures that the strategy is:

- Defined
- Agreed
- Maintained
- Achieved

The objectives of strategy management are to:

- Analyse the organisation's environment to identify opportunities;
- Identify constraints that could affect business outcomes;
- Decide and agree the organisation's perspective and direction, including vision, mission and principles;
- Establish the organisation's perspective and position with regard to customers and competitors;
- Ensure the strategy is translated into tactical and operational plans; and
- Manage changes to the strategy and related documents.

Strategy provides the overall direction for the organisation and is normally set at the senior management and governing body level. Strategy as a practice is evolving to become more fluid and less fixed; changes in technology, for example, can quickly invalidate a five-year plan.

Practice considerations

Strategy management can be challenging to understand for most employees because it requires executive involvement. If an attempt at 'strategy' is made at a lower level by junior employees, it will not have the authority needed and is more likely to fail.

Very reactive organisations will also find this a difficult practice to implement, if they allow short-term decisions to override the longer-term strategy. For example, an organisation that constantly defers to customers who demand specific solutions will find it difficult to follow a strategic path.

The measures applied to an organisation's strategy management capabilities must look at how well the strategy is integrated into the organisation as a whole. For example, is it reflected in the tactical and operational plans and procedures?

Supplier management

"The purpose of the supplier management practice is to ensure that the organization's suppliers and their performances are managed appropriately to support the seamless provision of quality products and services. This includes creating closer, more collaborative relationships with key suppliers to uncover and realize new value and reduce the risk of failure."

Supplier management activities include:

- Creating a single point of visibility and control to ensure consistency;
- Maintaining a supplier strategy and policy, and contract management information;
- Negotiating and agreeing contracts and arrangements;
- Managing relationships and contracts with internal and external suppliers; and
- Managing supplier performance.

The supplier strategy (often referred to as the sourcing strategy) defines the organisation's plan for how and where it will use suppliers. The options include:

- **Insourcing:** using resources internal to the organisation.
- **Outsourcing:** using external suppliers.
- **Single source or partnership:** procurement from a single supplier that supplies all elements of the service, or which acts as a service integrator to manage other suppliers on behalf of the organisation.
- **Multi-sourcing:** using more than one supplier.

Suppliers are selected and evaluated based on:

- Importance and impact
- Risk
- Costs

Supplier management process activities include:

- Supplier planning
- Evaluating suppliers and contracts
- Supplier and contract negotiation

- Supplier categorisation
- Supplier and contract management
- Warranty management
- Performance management
- Contract renewal and/or termination

Service integration and management

As organisations rely on more and more suppliers, it can prove challenging to manage them, particularly when things go wrong. Service integration and management (SIAM) is a management methodology that uses a service integrator role to coordinate service relationships across all suppliers.

Service integration and management might be done by staff within the organisation or by an external organisation.

🌐 **Practice considerations**

If your organisation doesn't already have a centralised supplier management practice, get ready to do some detective work. It's likely that individual teams and departments have been allowed to make their own agreements at the operational and commodity level, so there will be contracts throughout the organisation and no single point of ownership.

It's essential to start with a sound supplier management policy. This will set staff expectations about how they need to behave when selecting a new supplier, and why. Once this is in place, the situation will improve.

Some customers have found themselves trapped with a supplier or a contract that was negotiated in the past and just doesn't work. It's important to try to recover the situation as far as possible or check the cost of early termination if the relationship has broken down irrevocably.

If you're looking to enter into a contract with a supplier for all or part of service provision, be clear about exactly what you want. Too many contracts are based on a fuzzy understanding of what's needed, with extra services added at additional cost once the initial contract is in place. Getting the right agreement in place will save time, money and misery in the future.

Workforce and talent management

"The purpose of the workforce and talent management practice is to ensure that the organization has the right people with the appropriate skills and knowledge and in the correct roles to support its business objectives. The practice covers a broad set of activities focused on successfully engaging with the organization's employees and people resources, including planning, recruitment, onboarding, learning and development, performance measurement, and succession planning."

Workforce and talent management helps to make sure that an organisation has the right people in place to meet its strategic objectives and to support organisational velocity. Effective workforce and talent management will:

- Reduce backlogs
- Improve quality
- Avoid rework caused by defects
- Reduce wait times
- Close knowledge and skill gaps

Workforce and talent management supports the creation of an effective people strategy, which will help identify roles, knowledge, skills and attributes required by the organisation. It will also help make sure the organisation has appropriate personnel to support future growth and take advantage of opportunities.

The increasing use of external resources and suppliers as part of service delivery has led to a wider scope for workforce and talent management. Table 22 defines some of the key terms related to workforce and talent management.

Table 22: Workforce and Talent Management

Organisational velocity	*"The speed, effectiveness and efficiency with which an organization operates. Organizational velocity influences time to market, quality, safety, costs and risks."*
Competencies	*"The combination of observable and measurable knowledge, skills, abilities and attitudes that contribute to enhanced employee performance and ultimately result in organizational success."*
Skills	*"A developed proficiency or dexterity in thought, verbal communication or physical action."*
Knowledge	*"The understanding of facts or information acquired by a person through experience or education; the*

	theoretical or practical understanding of a subject."
Attitude	*"A set of emotions, beliefs, and behaviors towards a particular object, person, thing or event."*

Workforce and talent management activities include:

- Workforce planning
- Recruitment
- Performance measurement
- Personal development
- Learning and development
- Mentoring and succession planning

Practice considerations

Most ITSM professionals are 'knowledge workers' in the 'knowledge economy'. New ways of working need new ways of managing people, from recruitment through to development and reward systems.

Some of the considerations for workforce and talent management include:

- A move towards flexible/home working – do employees need to be on site? Does the company need an office? How do we communicate with and manage remote workers and virtual teams?
- What does productivity look like? Knowledge workers need space to think and to be creative, so standard productivity measures might not apply.

- How are we developing staff? Is a three-day training course once a year still effective? How do we encourage an attitude of continual personal development, and give people time to do it?

Notice the move from the language of 'human resources' to 'workforce and talent management'. Increasingly, the perception is that resources are 'dumb' things: money, computers, etc. If we treat our people as resources, they will behave like resources.

CHAPTER 13: SERVICE MANAGEMENT PRACTICES

Availability management

"The purpose of the availability management practice is to ensure that services deliver agreed levels of availability to meet the needs to customers and users."

Availability is defined as *"the ability of an IT service or other configuration item to perform its agreed function when required"*.

Availability management activities include:

- Negotiating and agreeing targets for availability;
- Designing infrastructure and applications to meet agreed levels;
- Ensuring that service and component data is collected to measure availability;
- Monitoring, analysing and reporting on availability; and
- Planning improvements to availability.

Availability is related to how often a service fails, and how quickly it can be recovered after a failure. These are often referred to as mean time between failure (MTBF) and mean time to restore service (MTRS).

Appropriate levels of availability need to be designed into each service. Technology changes including Software as a Service (SaaS) solutions and Cloud hosting platforms have led to significant increases in the availability of services.

Availability measurements could include:

- User outage minutes – incident duration multiplied by the number of users affected
- Number of lost transactions
- Business value lost
- User satisfaction

If failover or recovery mechanisms are used as part of service availability planning, these need to be tested regularly.

Practice considerations

Many organisations have tried to make the business case for availability management, only for the management team to tell them, 'Things are fine! Why should we spend any money?'

It's important to understand that just because things are OK today, it doesn't mean they'll be OK tomorrow. Sadly, the aftermath of a major incident, or availability loss, can be a great time to get funding and management attention for the implementation of availability management.

The actual definition of availability can also be tough. Services that are 'up' or 'down' are easy to identify, but what about intermittent availability, or degraded performance? Does that mean the service is available or not? The service provider organisation and the customer might have very different views here. Service level management and relationship management can help availability management to talk to the customer and get precise definitions for 'service up' and 'service down'.

Finally, remember that availability management can be complex and technical. Be very wary of customers who have heard a figure they like the sound of (for example, 99.999% or '5 9s') and ask for that as an availability target. It's sensible to check that the customer knows exactly what they are asking for and why – and if they are prepared to pay for the service. It can be a good idea to create a table to show your customer exactly what these figures mean in terms of minutes of downtime per week, month or year.

Business analysis

"The purpose of the business analysis practice is to analyze a business or some element of it, define its associated needs, and recommend solutions to address these needs and/or solve a business problem, which must facilitate value creation for stakeholders. Business analysis enables an organization to communicate its needs in a meaningful way, express the rationale for change, and design and describe solutions that enable value creation in alignment with the organization's objectives."

Business analysis takes a holistic view, considering:

- Process
- Organisation change
- Technology
- Policies
- Information
- Strategic planning

Business analysis activities include:

- Analysing business systems, processes, services and architectures;

- Identifying and prioritising improvements to the SVS, products and services;
- Identifying and prioritising opportunities for innovation;
- Evaluating and proposing actions to deliver improvement;
- Documenting business requirements to enable improvements; and
- Recommending solutions and validating them with stakeholders.

Process considerations

Business analysis is another area that is being affected by the shift to Agile working and the impact of digital transformation. Some organisations have adopted roles based on the Agile methodology, replacing business analysts with product owners. Other organisations are retaining the business analyst role but renaming it 'agile business analyst'.

Whatever the role is called, having an area of the organisation that is actively working to address business needs and identify opportunities for improvement is essential. Technology can provide huge advantages, but business users may not know how to articulate their requirements.

Capacity and performance management

"The purpose of the capacity and performance management practice is to ensure that services achieve agreed and expected performance, satisfying current and future demands in a cost-effective way."

Performance is defined as *"a measure of what is achieved or delivered by a system, person, team, practice or service"*.

Service performance is typically used to describe the number of service actions performed within a timeframe, and the time required to fulfil a service action at a given level of demand. Service performance relies on service capacity, which describes the maximum throughput of a service or service component.

Capacity and performance management activities include:

- Service performance and capacity analysis, including monitoring current performance and service modelling; and
- Service performance and capacity planning, including requirements analysis, demand forecasting and resource planning, and performance improvement planning.

Poor capacity and performance management capabilities can have a severe impact on service performance and, consequently, on customer satisfaction.

🌐 Practice considerations

Capacity and performance management is about more than just technology – it's about putting policies and procedures in place to govern capacity.

Business sponsors do not always respond well to requests from IT for more capacity investment (or to being asked to use less capacity). Increased access to home computing and the falling price of storage media both contribute to a 'just buy more space' attitude from the business. When implementing capacity and performance management, it's important to educate the business about the cost of capacity.

This isn't just the purchase price of storage, but the ongoing costs of housing, maintaining and backing up the data stored on it. This applies to both Cloud solutions and storage owned and managed by an organisation itself.

The information being stored by the business should be classified with a policy supporting sensible retention. Data can also be archived if it isn't regularly used, with access available on request.

Investment in capacity should be made 'just in time'. This means that capacity is bought when needed – it doesn't mean that it's bought at the last minute! If an organisation buys capacity too soon, it risks having idle, unused space. A delay in investment might benefit the organisation if the cost of technology falls significantly. If an organisation buys capacity too late, the performance of a service might have already been affected.

Cloud hosting services deliver significant benefits for capacity and performance management, providing scalable solutions that can be easily changed. They do, however, also introduce risks and need to be managed carefully to ensure ongoing value for money.

Change enablement

"The purpose of the change enablement practice is to maximize the number of successful service and product changes by ensuring that risks have been properly assessed, authorizing changes to proceed, and managing the change schedule."

"A change is the addition, modification, or removal of anything that could have a direct or indirect effect on services."

In ITIL, the person or group that authorises a change is referred to as the change authority. Change authority may be decentralised in organisations working at high speed and in agile environments, meaning peer review is more important and becomes an indicator of high performance. The change schedule is used to help plan changes, assist in communication, avoid conflicts and assign resources.

Change enablement must balance delivering benefits through successful changes and protecting live service from harmful changes.

Table 23 shows the change types:

Table 23: Types of Change

Standard change	Standard changes are low-risk, pre-authorised changes. They are well understood and documented so they can be implemented without additional authorisation. An example could be giving a new starter access to a piece of approved software.
Normal change	Normal changes need to be scheduled, assessed and authorised via the organisation's defined process. Lower-risk changes will need less scrutiny than high-risk changes. Many organisations have tools in place that manage change request

	workflows, automating the process where it makes sense to do so.
Emergency change	Emergency changes need to be implemented as soon as possible, perhaps in response to an issue or a security breach. They are assessed and authorised when possible, but some steps (e.g. testing) might be left out if the level of urgency justifies it. There may be a separate change authority for emergency changes.

Each organisation will define its own scope for change enablement. This often includes:

- IT infrastructure
- Applications
- Documentation
- Processes
- Supplier relationships
- Any other relevant areas

🌐 Practice considerations

It is very rare to find an organisation with no change enablement whatsoever. Most organisations have felt the pain of a failed change, or changes, and put in place some kind of process to try to stop it happening again. If you're looking at change enablement for your organisation, try to find out what already exists and see if you can build on that.

It is normal to face resistance to the introduction of more formal change oversight where there has been none before. Staff might feel they have to ask permission to do their job or perceive that their skills are being doubted. It's important to sell the benefits of change enablement and communicate that every change is linked and has the potential to affect service elsewhere.

You will really only have one chance with change enablement. Get it wrong, and any future efforts will be met with 'we tried that, and it was too bureaucratic/not effective', etc. Think carefully about the level of control that's actually needed – not too much and not too little.

The common response from technical teams during the implementation of change enablement is for them to ask 'What about x? Is x a change?' and 'What about z? Is z a change?'

The short answer is anything that can affect services or customers is a change. You can sell the process to staff by pointing out how it will protect them, as well as protecting services; if a change goes wrong, the organisation will look at the failings in the change enablement process, not at a particular team member's performance.

Agile/DevOps environments will often automate some/all of their change enablement. If code is being released frequently, an automated delivery pipeline with staged tests can ensure there is no impact on the live environment. If a test is failed, the code is pulled out. Automated change enablement must still generate logs of some kind to show what changes have been made, and the tests being used will need continual review.

Incident management

 "The purpose of the incident management practice is to minimize the negative impact of incidents by restoring normal service operation as quickly as possible."

An incident is *"an unplanned interruption to or reduction in the quality of a service"*.

Incidents need to be logged, prioritised and resolved within agreed timescales. They might be escalated to a support team for resolution, depending on the product or service affected and how quickly the resolution is required. Incident management needs to include quality, timely updates to the affected user(s), which requires a high level of collaboration between teams.

The incident management practice activities include:

- **Design the incident management practice:** the practice has to react appropriately to different incident types, depending on their impact. Major incidents and information security incidents might require special handling.
- **Prioritise incidents:** incidents with the highest impact and urgency need to be resolved first. Classifications and timescales are agreed with consumers.
- **Use an incident management tool to log and manage incidents:** the tool may provide links to changes, known errors and knowledge articles. It may also provide incident matching and links to problems.

Swarming

Some organisations use an incident management technique called swarming. A group of stakeholders work together until it becomes clear who is best placed to continue with the incident. Collaboration like this supports information sharing and provides learning opportunities within teams. This approach differs from traditional incident management practices, which escalate from first-line support teams to second-line, third-line, etc.

🌐 Practice considerations

In many organisations, incident management is the responsibility of the service desk, and the relationship between the service desk and second-line support teams may be poor. The service desk might see second-line support as being arrogant techies who bounce incidents back unnecessarily, won't talk to users and fix things in the order they feel like fixing them. Second-line support teams see the service desk as a nuisance, with unqualified staff who send poorly documented incidents that they could have fixed themselves. These relationship issues can be compounded when teams are part of different organisations (for example, second-line support is provided by an external organisation).

Neither of these opinions is entirely true!

Effective incident management can help to break down the barriers between the teams. Incident models (contributed to by second-line staff) make sure the right data is recorded and the incident is sent to the right place. Timescales and priorities make sure incidents are fixed in the right order, with no argument about what should be done first.

Incident management is often an ideal candidate for automation, and many mature tools exist for this process. When selecting a tool, look for ease-of-use functionality, e.g. integration with phone systems, the ability to auto-populate fields and excellent reporting.

Incident management can really help to build buy-in for a service management implementation. It can provide fast improvements for end users along with brilliant management information for IT. If you can start with a practice that delivers results quickly, it can be easier to make a case for investment in other service management processes.

One area that trips up a lot of organisations is the level of categorisation they introduce. Keep it simple, and control which roles are allowed to add categories. The category trees in some organisations have hundreds and hundreds of entries when actually a few dozen would do the job. Be very wary of introducing a 'misc' or 'unknown' category – you might find everything ends up there.

IT asset management

"The purpose of the IT asset management practice is to plan and manage the full lifecycle of all IT assets, to help the organization to:

- *Maximize value*
- *Control costs*
- *Manage risks*
- *Support decision making about purchase, reuse, retirement and disposal of assets*
- *Meet regulatory and contractual requirements."*

An IT asset is *"any financially valuable component that can contribute to the delivery of an IT product or service"*.

The scope of asset management will usually include:

- Software
- Hardware
- Networking
- Cloud services
- Client devices

It might also include non-IT assets that are part of service delivery, for example a data centre where IT assets are housed.

Types of asset management include:

- IT asset management (ITAM)
- Software asset management (SAM)
- Hardware asset management (HAM)

IT asset management relies on accurate asset information, which is held in an asset register. Some organisations capture this information in a one-off exercise (an audit, or a stocktake-type exercise), but it's better to update the information in the asset register regularly, using inputs from service management practices like release management that are involved with changes of asset states.

IT asset management activities vary according to the asset type:

- **For hardware assets:** labelling, location tracking, lifecycle management through to disposal in line with any relevant regulations or legislation.
- **For software assets:** protection from unlicensed use, licence tracking and management, lifecycle management.
- **Cloud-based assets:** role management for users with access to Cloud assets, licence and information security management where relevant, cost management.
- **Client assets:** recording the individuals who own assets, lifecycle management and management of data on client devices.

The practice activities include:

- Defining, populating and maintaining the asset register;
- Providing storage facilities for assets and related media;
- Controlling asset lifecycles;
- Providing reports and data about assets as required; and
- Auditing assets as required, providing data for external audit activities.

Practice considerations

Asset management (and particularly software asset management) is a practice with a very strong business case. A good software asset manager can save an organisation many thousands of dollars in licence fees and help them avoid the significant costs associated with non-compliance.

This is a very specialised area, and if your organisation is just starting out with asset management, I recommend you get external advice. SAM consultants will have licence models and suppliers with which they are particularly experienced, and it is often cheaper and easier to use their experience than to go through the learning curve yourself.

The introduction of Cloud services like Amazon Web Services (AWS) and Microsoft Azure has created new challenges for service management professionals. Some of the technical elements of service management (overall capacity and availability planning, for example) now sit with the Cloud services provider, but cost management, information security and access management still sit with the client organisation. I recommend supplier-specific training as well as doing your own online research if you're responsible for Cloud services or are integrating these into your service management model.

Monitoring and event management

"The purpose of the monitoring and event management practice is to systematically observe services and service components, and record and report selected changes of state identified as events. This practice identifies and prioritizes infrastructure, services, business processes, and information security events, and establishes the appropriate response to those events, including responding to conditions that could lead to potential faults or incidents."

An event is *"any change of state that has significance for the management of a service or other configuration item. Events are typically recognized through notifications created by an IT service, configuration item or monitoring tool. "*

This practice manages events through their lifecycle to prevent, minimise or eliminate any negative impact they might have. Monitoring focuses on observing services and service components to detect any potentially significant state changes or conditions. This is almost always done using automation. Event management focuses on recording and managing the outputs from monitoring that are classified as events. Each event will be assessed, and the correct control action initiated. A control action might be 'do nothing', continue monitoring, or initiate another practice like incident management. Not all the outputs from monitoring become events.

Events are classified in one of three ways:

- **Informational** – no action required, but may form part of a trend or data for analysis.
- **Warning** – action needs to be taken to avoid negative impact.
- **Exception** – action required; negative business impact might already have occurred.

As well as classifying events, monitoring and event management processes and procedures must address:

- Identifying what to monitor;
- Implementing and maintaining monitoring;
- Establishing and maintaining thresholds and criteria to identify and classify events;
- Establishing and maintaining policies for event management; and

- Implementing and improving processes and automation for monitoring and event management.

Although much of the monitoring and event management activities are automated, human intervention is still essential. Organisations will use a mix of in-built monitoring capabilities in service components, custom monitoring tools, and human intervention and oversight.

🌐 Practice considerations

I've seen monitoring and event management implementations go wrong in two main ways. The first is when not enough information is collected. Even though processes are in place, tools aren't picking up the right events and service is still being affected. This makes it very hard to justify further investment in the process.

The second is when too much information is collected and passed to operations teams; they end up swamped and start to ignore events – even the important ones. The process needs to constantly refine what is being collected and where it is sent, to make sure the important information is not missed.

When implementing monitoring and event management, it's best to start with a simple set of measures, and then add to them as the practice matures. Incidents and problems can be used as learning opportunities to identify whether further monitoring would be beneficial.

It's also very important to publicise the success of monitoring and event management. Because the practice works proactively and can prevent incidents before they occur, there's a danger that its successes are rarely seen outside of operations. If monitoring and event management is proactively preventing incidents and improving the level of service on offer, this should be used to justify further investment.

Problem management

📋 *"The purpose of the problem management practice is to reduce the likelihood and impact of incidents by identifying actual and potential causes of incidents and managing workarounds and known errors."*

"A problem is a cause, or potential cause, of one or more incidents."

Problems require investigation and analysis to identify the causes, develop workarounds, and recommend longer-term resolution to reduce the number and impact of future incidents.

"A workaround is a solution that reduces or eliminates the impact of an incident or problem for which a full resolution is not yet available. Some workarounds reduce the likelihood of incidents."

Workarounds are documented in problem records, and then reviewed and improved as problem analysis progresses. A workaround can be as simple as asking a user to reboot a PC.

"A known error is a problem that has been analyzed but not yet resolved."

Known errors are documented and made available to other practices, for example, the service desk.

Figure 12 shows the three phases of problem management:

Figure 12: The phases of problem management[12]

Problem identification activities identify and log problems. They include:

- Trend analysis of data including incident records;
- Detecting recurring issues;
- Identifying whether major incidents might recur;
- Working with suppliers and partners; and
- Analysing information from developers, testing and project teams.

Problem control activities include:

- Problem analysis, prioritisation and management based on risk;
- Documenting workarounds; and
- Documenting known errors.

Error control activities include:

- Identifying potential permanent solutions;

---

[12] *ITIL® Foundation, ITIL 4 edition*, figure 5.23.

- Ongoing management and reassessment of known errors; and
- Ongoing management and improvement of workarounds.

Problem management interfaces with other practices including change enablement and incident management as part of its role.

🌐 Practice considerations

Problem management needs to be implemented carefully. If it is set up as a separate team or group, there is a danger it will just become a dumping ground for everything the other support staff find too difficult – similar to the issues often experienced by 'continual improvement' teams.

Problem management should be viewed as a point of coordination for investigation and resolution of problems. Its role is to work with multiple support teams at once, making sure investigation is carried out in a sensible way and actions are documented so they are not duplicated.

Sometimes an organisation will experience a problem that no one wants to take responsibility for. The network team will insist it's a server issue, and the server team will insist it's an application fault. In this situation, problem management needs to have the authority to get the teams to work together, eliminating possible causes until the true cause is identified. In a multi-supplier environment, a service integrator might need to be involved with problem management across the supply chain.

Many organisations struggle to differentiate between incidents and problems. It is essential to define and clearly communicate the scope of the two practices. Just because an incident has been open for a long time doesn't make it a problem.

Service management tools can significantly improve the performance and usefulness of problem management. If workarounds are easily searchable and problems can be linked to incident records, the practice will work well. If it's too hard to find a workaround, the incident management staff won't bother, and problem management won't deliver value.

You don't need to have a mature incident management practice and lots of incident records to do problem management. If your incident records are poor, I recommend conducting a user and IT staff survey to find out what they think the top ten recurring incidents are, and work from that.

Release management

"The purpose of the release management practice is to make new and changed services and features available for use."

A release is *"a version of a service or other configuration item, or a collection of configuration items, that is made available for use"*.

A release can include:

- Infrastructure components
- Application components
- Documentation
- Training
- Updated or new processes
- Updated or new tools

- Any other required components

Releases may be very minor (for example, one changed feature) or major, such as a new service. A release plan is used to describe the release, release timing and its components. The release schedule then documents the exact timing for releases, based on times that have been negotiated and agreed with customers where necessary. After a release, a post-implementation review is carried out to identify learning and improvement opportunities, and to make sure customers are satisfied with the release outcomes.

Release management activities will be different in waterfall and Agile environments.

Table 24: Release Management Activities – Agile and Waterfall

Agile	Release management activity may take place after deployment, which is delivered in small increments.
Waterfall	Most planning work is done before the release. Deployment and release management activities may be combined into a single process.

Release management may be 'big bang' with all changes taking place at once, or 'staged', with pilot releases used to test the release before the full rollout.

In a DevOps environment, release management may be integrated into a continuous integration/continuous delivery toolchain. Releases will often contain components provided by external suppliers, so release management needs to work across organisational boundaries.

Practice considerations

Release management relies on effective design activities. If the product or service design has not defined a transition approach, remedial release management work will be needed to make suitable decisions about how to deploy the new or changed product or service.

Release management also requires close links with change enablement, IT asset management and configuration management. Change enablement provides authorisation for release activities, and configuration management provides information to support planning.

In many organisations, I've seen situations where release build and test activities are not allocated enough time and resources in the project plan. Once development is complete, these organisations' normal way of working is to rush the release, worrying about testing, training and documentation once it has gone live. This is obviously not acceptable and, if this is the case, cultural change may also be required to change the priority from meeting a deadline to delivering a quality product.

Release management will be more challenging in an environment with one or more external suppliers involved in service delivery. It is important to make sure that external suppliers align with any release policies implemented within the organisation and to track their compliance.

The organisational attitude to early life support can also affect release management. Early life support should end when operations confirm they will accept the service, because it is performing as it should. In many organisations, early life support is defined by a time period, not by quality standards. Early life support ends after (for example) two weeks, whether the service is performing well or not. This can lead to a rift between transition and operation staff. Early life support must be based around service performance, not time.

The challenges associated with release management (and many other service management practices) will evolve as technology evolves. Cloud computing and SaaS may make the process simpler, if applications are hosted centrally. Bring your own device (BYOD) gives users more control of the hardware they access services from, and so will make the process more complicated.

Service catalogue management

"The purpose of the service catalogue management practice is to provide a single source of consistent information on all services and service offerings, and to ensure that it is available to the relevant audience."

The service catalogue contains a list of services that are available to customers (a subset of the information in the service portfolio). The catalogue might be a document or spreadsheet, an online portal or a sophisticated tool; the important functionality is to be able to communicate the right information to its users.

Service catalogue management activities include publishing, updating and editing service and product descriptions and any related information. More sophisticated service catalogues will offer 'views' of data depending on the role of the person viewing the catalogue:

- **User view** – shows information about services and how to request them.
- **Customer view** – adds service level, financial and performance data.
- **IT to IT customer view** – shows technical, information security and process information for use in service delivery.
- **Request catalogue** – shows service requests associated with services, and allows requests for new and existing services.

Practice considerations

It is hard to implement a service catalogue and, once it's been implemented, it can be hard to keep the information in it up to date.

Service catalogue implementation must start with a clear definition of what a 'service' actually is. The service provider organisation must consult its customers during this stage – their view of the services provided may be radically different from what the service provider organisation thinks it provides. Where consultation with consumers is not possible, the service catalogue may develop iteratively over time as feedback from consumers is received.

Once the high-level services have been agreed and the service catalogue is populated, it needs to be kept up to date. Service catalogue management needs to link to practices including change enablement and service portfolio management to help it to do this. If these practices are not in place, service catalogue management will have to work much harder to keep track of service changes and updates.

Don't rush straight in and buy an expensive toolset as part of the process implementation. Service catalogues often start as a simple spreadsheet or matrix, before evolving to views that are more complex. It's the information in the catalogue and its accessibility that's important – not the fanciness of the tool used to support it.

Service configuration management

"The purpose of the service configuration management practice is to ensure that accurate and reliable information about the configuration of services, and the configuration items that support them, is available when and where it is needed. This includes information on how configuration items are configured and the relationships between them."

A configuration item (CI) is *"any component that needs to be managed in order to deliver an IT service".*

Service configuration management collects and manages information about CIs including:

- Hardware
- Software
- Networks
- Buildings
- People
- Suppliers
- Documentation
- Services

Service configuration management differs from IT asset management because it collects information on the CIs that support each service (often using data from IT asset management as one of its sources) and the relationships between them. Figure 13 shows an example of a simplified service model for an IT service.

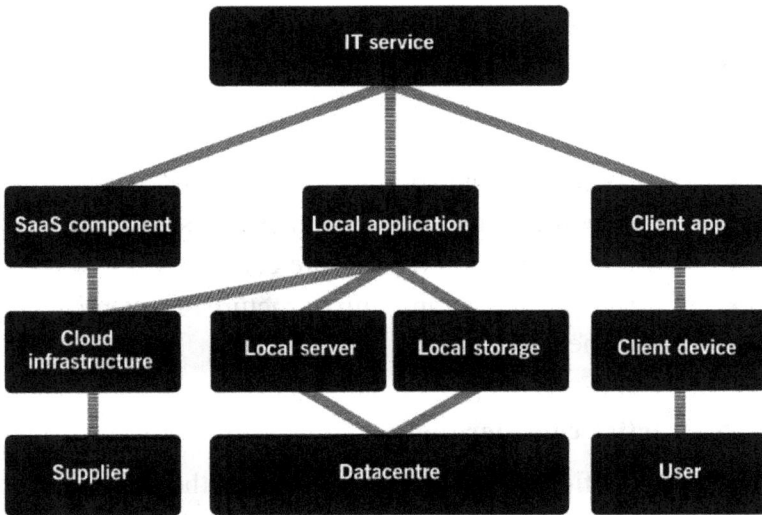

Figure 13: Simplified service model for a typical IT service[13]

The value provided by service configuration management is indirect; it achieves most value when other practices are using the information it supplies. The effort and cost

---

[13] *ITIL® Foundation, ITIL 4 edition*, figure 5.29.

associated with collecting configuration data must be balanced against the benefit realised by having the data.

Configuration information needs to be stored in a controlled way, often in a configuration management system (CMS). The CMS is a *"set of tools, data and information that is used to support service configuration management"*. Ideally, the CMS will be part of the same toolset or have interfaces to the tools used by other practices, such as incident management and change enablement.

Configuration management needs to be able to:

- Identify new CIs and add them to the CMS;
- Update configuration data when changes are made;
- Verify configuration records are correct; and
- Audit applications and infrastructure to identify any undocumented CIs.

Practice considerations

Service configuration management is, theoretically, an essential capability for service management, because it underpins and supports so many other service management practices. How can we manage our infrastructure if we don't know what we've got, where it is or if it's working? However, in reality, there are many service provider organisations with incomplete configuration management information – because it's seen as too complicated, or the business case for configuration management is not clear.

It's likely that there will be some asset or configuration management happening in parts of your organisation already. See what exists, and whether you can use anything that's already in place.

Major projects can be a good opportunity to implement service configuration management. If there's (for example) an office move or hardware refresh happening, that's a good time to start collecting data and develop a baseline. Once you have this information, the focus moves to keeping it up to date.

The business case for service configuration management will always focus on indirect, rather than direct, process benefits. Think about how much quicker incidents could be resolved, or how many more successful changes there might be. These are where you will really see the process add value.

It's very unusual to find service configuration management implemented in isolation. Normally, it will be implemented in conjunction with, or after, change enablement and release management. Without change enablement, there is very little hope of keeping the CMS up to date.

Service continuity management

"The purpose of the service continuity management practice is to ensure that the availability and performance of a service are maintained at sufficient levels in the case of a disaster. The practice provides a framework for building organizational resilience with the capability of providing an effective response that safeguards the interests of key stakeholders and the organization's reputation, brand and value-creating activities."

Service continuity management supports overall business continuity management (BCM) and planning, by making sure IT and IT services can be resumed following a disaster or a crisis. It is triggered by a disruption or risk that is outside the scope of normal response practices like incident and problem management.

Each organisation needs to define what 'disaster' means to it. The Business Continuity Institute defines a disaster as "a sudden unplanned event that causes great damage or serious loss to an organization. It results in an organization failing to provide critical business functions for some predetermined period of time."

Disaster sources could be:

- Supply chain failure
- Terrorism
- Weather
- Cyber attack
- Political event

They can affect any of an organisation's stakeholders, and their impact can include:

- Loss of income
- Reputational damage
- Breach of regulations/fines
- Loss of market share
- Insolvency

Table 25 shows some key definitions for service continuity management.

Table 25: Key Definitions for Service Continuity Management

Recovery time objective (RTO)	*"The maximum acceptable period of time following a service disruption that can elapse before the lack of business functionality severely impacts the organization. This represents the maximum agreed time within which a product or an activity must be resumed, or resources must be recovered."*
Recovery point objective (RPO)	*"The point to which information used by an activity must be restored to enable the activity to operate on resumption."*
Disaster recovery plans	*"A set of clearly defined plans related to how an organization will recover from a disaster as well as return to a pre-disaster condition, considering the four dimensions of service management."*
Business impact analysis (BIA)	*"A key activity in the practice of service continuity management that identifies vital business functions (VBFs) and their dependencies. These dependencies may include suppliers, people, other business processes, and IT services. BIA defines the recovery requirements for IT services. These requirements include*

	RTOs, RPOs, and minimum target service levels for each IT service."

🌐 Practice considerations

Service continuity management is another service management practice that often starts with a blaze of glory. Ironically, the best time to get funding to start this process is directly after a period of extreme disruption, when the business realises what it has to lose and why it needs to plan (in a similar way to availability management).

In the initial excitement, consultants will be hired, and documents drawn up, but organisations also need to plan for what happens when the consultants leave.

Has a practice owner been put in place? Is there a genuine commitment to the process? Will ongoing testing be seen as a priority, or gradually dropped in favour of the day job?

The level of commitment to service continuity management will always be linked to the type of organisation and the markets in which it operates. If the organisation operates in a risk-averse, time-critical, heavily regulated market, it is much more likely to invest in service continuity management. Imagine a bank having a service loss and saying 'sorry, we can't recover your information'. In fact, you might have seen stories very similar to this make the news!

Service continuity management also tends to become more of a concern as organisations mature. Immature organisations are usually much more focused on day-to-day activities and just hope things won't happen. Mature organisations will consider the risks more carefully and start to plan for when things go wrong. As organisations grow, they may fall within the scope of legislation and regulation that requires them to have more formal service continuity management in place.

Service design

"The purpose of the service design practice is to design products and services that are fit for purpose, fit for use, and that can be delivered by the organization and its ecosystem. This includes planning and organizing people, partners and suppliers, information, communication, technology, and practices for new or changed products and services, and the interaction between the organization and its customers."

Poor design leads to services and products that don't meet customer needs or facilitate value creation. Many organisations follow an iterative and incremental approach to service design, to allow products and services to continually adapt as organisational and customer requirements evolve.

Poor service design can lead to products and services that are expensive to run, don't operate as expected, and don't meet customer needs. Improvement programmes may only be able to patch over the cracks; effective design can get things right first time. Service design needs to focus on customer experience (CX) and user experience (UX). This can be achieved by involving customers and users in the design process, and will lead to:

- Customer-centric products and services;
- A holistic approach to service design;
- Better estimates for design projects (time, cost, resources, etc.);

- Higher volumes of successful changes;
- Creation of effective, reusable design methods;
- Increased confidence in the ability to deliver new or changed products and services; and
- Maintainable and effective products and services.

Holistic service design needs to consider:

- Other products and services
- All relevant stakeholders
- Existing architectures
- Technology (current and future required)
- Service management practices and processes
- Measurements and metrics

Design thinking

Design thinking is a *"practical and human-centred approach that accelerates innovation"*. Design thinking activities include:

- Inspiration and empathy, through observation of people, how they work and how they interact with products and services;
- Ideation, which combines divergent and convergent thinking;
- Prototyping, to test, iterate and refine ideas;
- Implementation, to bring concepts to life; and
- Evaluation, to measure performance and identify opportunities for improvement.

🌐 Practice considerations

Product and service design practices have benefited from a lot of attention and innovation in recent years. Evolving ways of working (for example, Agile software development) have changed the way organisations approach design activities. Maintaining a focus on customer and user experience forces design teams to walk in their customers' shoes.

Service design is more effective when there is input from many different stakeholders, including support teams, customers, users and suppliers. Consider where design activities are taking place in your organisation and challenge any siloed approaches to service design.

Lessons to be learned from design projects can be lost if teams are broken up and quickly reassigned to new work, so if possible, I recommend adding a learning activity to each design project before people move on to new activities. As lessons are learned and shared, good design practices will become automatic. DevOps thinking encourages keeping the same people involved in the design and running of products and services; this is also a way to make sure knowledge stays within the team.

The service desk

📋 *"The purpose of the Service Desk practice is to capture demand for incident resolution and service requests. It should also be the entry point and single point of contact for the service provider with all of its users."*

The service desk will capture and funnel demand, including:

- **Acknowledge:** the user needs to know that their contact has been received; for example, issues reported via email could receive an auto-acknowledgement.
- **Classify:** classification helps the service desk to understand what it is dealing with and how important it is.
- **Own:** ownership ensures no issue or request gets 'lost' between teams or systems.
- **Act:** resolving things to the user's satisfaction.

Possible service desk channels include:

- Telephone
- Service portals
- Mobile applications
- Live chat and chatbots
- Email
- Walk-in
- Text messages and social media messaging
- Public and private discussion forums

Service desks may be centralised or virtual:

- **Virtual:** agents can work from multiple locations, using technology to allow them to collaborate.
- **Centralised:** the service desk is a team working in a single location.

Some service desk staff are very technical, whereas others are less technical and work more closely with technical teams within the organisation. Service desk staff skills include:

- Empathy

- Emotional intelligence
- Effective communication
- Customer service skills
- Understanding of business priority, incident analysis and prioritisation

Technologies that support service desks include:

- Intelligent telephony systems
- Workforce management/resource planning systems
- Call recording and quality control
- Dashboard and monitoring tools
- Workflow systems
- Knowledge base
- Remote access tools
- Configuration management systems

🌐 Practice considerations

Organisational attitudes to the service desk can be surprising. On one hand, it's the 'shop window' of the organisation and vitally important that users get a good experience. On the other hand, staff can work long hours under pressure, in poorly paid roles with little opportunity for advancement.

If your service desk is important to your organisation, the staff who work there need to be treated with respect. Many people use a service desk role as a way to access jobs in the IT industry – it's a great place to learn about IT quickly before advancing to other roles. Where possible, I recommend allowing service desk staff to rotate and spend time with other teams, and having clear progression plans in place for people to move away from the service desk. This allows them to progress their careers without the organisation losing all of their valuable knowledge.

Organisations like the Service Desk Institute (SDI) and HDI (formerly the Helpdesk Institute) provide support, resources and events for service desk and support staff.

Service level management

"The purpose of the service level management practice is to set clear business-based targets for service levels, and to ensure that delivery of services is properly assessed, monitored, and managed against those targets."

A service level is *"one or more metrics that define expected or achieved service quality"*.

A service level agreement is *"a documented agreement between a service provider and a customer that identifies both services required and the expected level of service"*.

Service level agreements (SLAs) are used to measure the service performance from the customer's point of view.

Successful SLAs need to:

- Be related to a defined service so the scope is clear;
- Relate to outcomes, not just operational metrics like '99% availability';
- Reflect an agreement between the customer and service provider organisation; and
- Be simple to read and understand.

Service level management provides end-to-end visibility of an organisation's services:

- It establishes a shared view of services and target service levels.
- It collects, analyses, stores and reports on relevant metrics.
- It performs service reviews and identifies improvement opportunities.
- It captures and reports on service issues.

Key skills for service level management include:

- Relationship management
- Business liaison
- Business analysis
- Supplier management

Service level management will collect information from:

- Business metrics, which measure business activities such as making a sale, or processing an invoice;
- Operational metrics, which help build a picture of overall performance and whether outcomes are being met;
- Customer feedback, including surveys and defined business-related measures; and
- Customer engagement, including initial conversations and listening, discovery and information capture, measurement and ongoing process discussions, and asking simple, open-ended questions.

Practice considerations

Service level management (SLM) isn't something that an organisation can implement as a project and then forget about. SLAs need to be reviewed and kept up to date as the organisation grows and services change. Many organisations hire consultants to help them implement SLM, because this gives them access to the consultant's skills and templates. Once the consultants leave, the documents are dropped into a cupboard, or online document store, and not referenced again. Implementing successful SLM means putting the processes in place to manage the agreements, not just creating documents.

It is also tempting to create huge SLAs that are complex, wordy and cover every eventuality – don't! Start simply – more information can be added later if needed.

SLAs need to represent consensus between the service provider organisation and its consumers. If one side doesn't engage with the process, it will fail. For example, in some organisations, customers try to implement SLAs to control a service provider organisation or function they perceive to be failing, but the service provider may simply ignore the targets.

For some services (for example, a Cloud hosting service), the organisation providing the service offers only standard options, with no option for customers to modify or adapt the SLA. Here, the consumer has a simple choice: to accept the SLA or not.

Finally, be clear about what SLM is trying to achieve. Some service provider organisations will adopt an 'easy' set of targets that they know they can deliver, even if failures occur. They are frightened that if they fail a target, they will be punished. Accept that targets will be breached – but this is an opportunity for improvement, not to have a fight.

Service request management

"The purpose of the service request management practice is to support the agreed quality of a service by handling all pre-defined, user-initiated service requests in an effective and user-friendly manner."

A service request is *"a request from a user or a user's authorized representative that initiates a service action which has been agreed as a normal part of service delivery"*.

Service requests are different from incidents because they are part of normal service delivery. Nothing has failed. They are handled using predefined and pre-agreed procedures, liaising with change enablement where necessary.

Common types of service request include:

- Request for a service delivery action
- Request for information
- Request for provision of a resource or service
- Request for access to a resource or service
- Feedback, compliments and complaints

Successful service request management relies on these considerations:

- Service request management should be automated and standardised as much as possible.
- Continual improvement should be applied to service request management.
- Policies should be used to allow requests to be fulfilled with appropriate authorisation.
- User expectations should be clearly set.

- Requests that are actually incidents or changes need to be redirected to the appropriate practice.

Service requests can have simple or complex workflows. The steps in the workflows should be well-known and proven. The service provider organisation will agree fulfilment times and provide clear status communication to users. Some service requests can be fulfilled via self-service; for example, requesting a new piece of software or access to a printer.

Practice considerations

As with many service management practices, when you implement service request management (SRM), keep it simple. Most end users have some experience of Internet shopping, which will help them understand the concept of ordering things via a web page. However, if your users only have basic IT literacy, keep things as simple as possible.

The request models you define will be very helpful when you create your workflows and user interface for SRM. For example, you might be able to create one simple request template for 'new user', rather than expecting your requestor to know exactly what type of chair, desk, mouse, mouse mat, keyboard, base unit, monitor, etc. to ask for.

When it comes to SRM within your own organisation, you need management support and you need your managers to walk the walk. It's no use trying to force everyone down a central process, if your management team are walking round with the latest shiny toys they paid for out of their own budget. If the organisational decision is that SRM offers two types of laptop as standard, that's what your management team need to be using.

The SRM workflows will also need to get the right level of approval in the right place. If a line manager has to sign off a mobile device for a user, this authorisation has to be granted before procurement can start. If you don't manage authorisation carefully, you might find you've spent a lot of money and aren't able to recoup it from the business.

Service validation and testing

🌐 *"The purpose of the service validation and testing practice is to ensure that new or changed products and services meet defined requirements. The definition of service value is based on input from customers, business objectives, and regulatory requirements, and is documented as part of the value chain activity of design and transition. These inputs are used to establish measurable quality and performance indicators that support the definition of assurance criteria and testing requirements."*

Service validation focuses on the creation and agreement of deployment and release management acceptance criteria. These will address utility and warranty, and must be based on customer requirements. The acceptance criteria are then measured via testing, based on the organisation's test strategy.

Test types can include:

- Utility/functional tests
  - o Unit test
  - o System test
  - o Integration test
  - o Regression test
- Warranty/non-functional tests
  - o Performance and capacity tests

o Security test
o Compliance test
o Operational test

Practice considerations

The independence of testing is crucial. It's good practice to use separate resources for development and testing of a new or changed service where practical. Developers know what a service is meant to do, so may be able to work around unexpected results in ways a user could not. They might also be tempted to ignore failures in favour of meeting a deadline.

The test environment is an area that requires careful consideration. It needs to reflect the live environment, so it must be updated when changes are approved and implemented. This needs to be considered when the scope of change management is being agreed.

Data in the test environment must be protected in the same way that live data is, and licensing also needs to be addressed – some software vendors provide licences for test environments free of charge, but others do not.

From an operations perspective, the test environment can look like an extension of the spares storage area. When a piece of the live infrastructure breaks, it's tempting to grab something from the test environment that isn't currently in use. This is dangerous. The test environment must be protected so that the testing carried out delivers valid results.

CHAPTER 14: TECHNICAL MANAGEMENT PRACTICES

Deployment management

📋 *"The purpose of the deployment management practice is to move new or changed hardware, software, documentation, processes, or any other component to live environments. It may also be involved in deploying components to other environments for testing or staging."*

🌐 Deployment management works closely with release management and change enablement. There are several deployment approaches; organisations will choose an appropriate approach depending on the nature of the release or releases:

- **Phased deployment** – deploys to part of the organisation or target group (for example, an office, or a country) each time, rather than the whole organisation at once.
- **Continuous delivery** – components are integrated, tested and deployed as needed, typically with an automated pipeline.
- **Big bang deployment** – the deployment is delivered to the whole organisation or target group at the same time.
- **Pull deployment** – users can download the software when they choose to.

Components need to be secured before deployment to protect their integrity. ITIL refers to these locations (whether physical or virtual) as the definitive media library and the definitive hardware store.

🌐 Practice considerations

Deployment management is often only visible when something goes wrong. When an organisation's IT services make the news, it's often blamed on a deployment not performing as expected.

A failed deployment can have a significant impact on customer and user satisfaction, so putting some simple controls in place will lead to big benefits. Protecting the integrity of components before a deployment will include looking at levels of access and the audit trails that are in place, both internally and across any relevant external suppliers.

The technology available to support deployment management is becoming more and more sophisticated. I recommend regularly reviewing the tools used by your organisation to make sure you're getting the best from them, and to identify where technological advances could be applied.

Infrastructure and platform management

🌐 *"The purpose of the infrastructure and platform management practice is to oversee the infrastructure and platforms used by an organization. When carried out properly, this practice enables the monitoring of technology solutions available to the organization, including the technology of external service providers."*

IT infrastructure includes physical and/or virtual technology resources, for example:

- Servers
- Storage
- Networks
- Client hardware
- Middleware
- Operating systems

These provide the environments that support the delivery of IT services. Infrastructure and platform management includes provision of technology to support value-creating activities and adopting to new technologies as they emerge. Each organisation needs to create its own infrastructure and platform management strategy to meet consumer needs, both now and in the future.

🌐 Practice considerations

Infrastructure and platform management (often seen as the responsibility of IT operations) has evolved enormously in recent years. Application developers used to grumble that operations teams were too slow in giving them access to the environments that they needed, with new servers and new platforms being built using manual processes.

Some of the most important changes related to infrastructure and platform management are Operations as a Service (OaaS), site reliability engineering (SRE), and advances in technology.

OaaS describes how an operations team or an external supplier will work with development teams to create environments that meet their needs fully. The team that is offering OaaS will carry out all the environment administration, including security, backups, capacity management, etc. OaaS vendors are emerging that offer specialised capabilities in this area.

SRE was pioneered by Google and describes using software engineering techniques in operations to create scalable and reliable systems.

Access to advances in technology including Cloud hosting and containers can also make infrastructure and platform management more effective and much faster.

Software development and management

"The purpose of the software development and management practice is to ensure that applications meet internal and external stakeholder needs, in terms of functionality, reliability, maintainability, compliance and auditability."

Software can describe anything from a single program to a larger suite of programs, for example, an operating environment. Software development and management ensures that software is fit for purpose and for use. Its activities include:

- Solution architecture
- Solution design
- Software development
- Software testing

- Provision and management of code repositories or libraries
- Package creation
- Version control, sharing and management of code

Most software development follows either waterfall or Agile ways of working. Software development and management is a continually evolving practice, with ways of working that adapt as technology adapts.

🌐 Practice considerations

If you want to know how effective your organisation's software development and management practices are, you don't need to look much further than your last few new products or services. Were they delivered on time? On budget? Did they meet the customer's requirements?

We've already discussed how new approaches to software development like Agile are creating benefits for organisations, as well as bringing challenges such as integrating Agile ways of working with business processes like financial management.

My main recommendation here is to shift your thinking so that you no longer consider software development a finite project with a beginning and an end. Even when a new piece of software is released, it's not 'finished'. Effective software development and management includes monitoring live products and services and continually improving them.

CHAPTER 15: SERVICE MANAGEMENT TRAINING AND QUALIFICATIONS

Service management can only be successful if staff have the right skills to do their job. Staff who don't have the right skills may feel demotivated and won't understand how their role contributes to the value that the customer receives. As services change and evolve, staff may need training or different roles to evolve with them. Skills may also be sourced from external organisations that provide support for relevant activities.

Service management depends on trained, motivated and experienced staff. Staff need to understand business priorities, and how IT supports them. They need customer service skills and the ability and opportunity to innovate. Staff need to be willing to follow and improve processes and procedures.

Many ITIL roles share generic requirements. These include:

- Management skills
- Meeting-management skills
- Communication skills – both written and verbal
- Negotiation skills
- An analytical mind

Service management staff and skill sets can be managed more easily, if standard roles and job titles are used. Many organisations are adopting frameworks such as the Skills Framework for the Information Age to help assign skills to roles. You can read more about the skills framework at _www.sfia.org.uk_.

From a service management perspective, training helps a service provider organisation and its staff to improve and demonstrate its capabilities. Approved ITIL training, via the official qualification scheme, is a quality-controlled way for service provider organisations to develop their staff. This will deliver personal and organisational benefits.

The ITIL qualification scheme

Figure 14 shows the ITIL 4 qualification scheme.

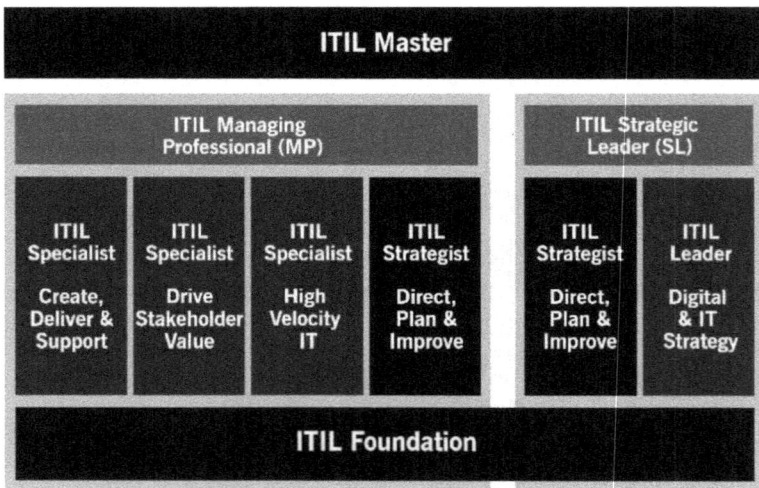

Figure 14: The ITIL 4 qualification scheme[14]

---

[14] *ITIL® Foundation, ITIL 4 edition*, "The ITIL 4 qualification scheme".

Starting with the ITIL Foundation is mandatory for any learner who wishes to advance to higher-level ITIL studies. Previous versions of the ITIL Foundation certificate can also be used to fulfil this prerequisite.

Above the Foundation level, the ITIL 4 certification scheme has two streams: ITIL Managing Professional (ITIL MP) and ITIL Strategic Leader (ITIL SL).

The ITIL MP stream provides practical and technical knowledge about how to run successful IT projects, teams and workflows, and is for IT practitioners working within technology and digital teams across businesses. This stream is made up of four courses:

- Create, Deliver & Support
- Drive Stakeholder Value
- High Velocity IT
- Direct, Plan & Improve

The first three courses are ITIL Specialist modules, and Direct, Plan & Improve is an ITIL Strategist module.

All the courses have individual benefits, but to certify as an ITIL MP, the Foundation and all four courses in the stream must be completed.

The ITIL SL stream recognises the value of ITIL, not just for IT, but for all digital (or IT-enabled) services. This stream is made up of two courses:

- ITIL Strategist Direct, Plan & Improve
- ITIL Leader Digital & IT Strategy

The ITIL Master then provides another level of ITIL certification.

CHAPTER 16: MULTIPLE-CHOICE EXAM STRATEGIES

The ITIL Foundation exam is:

- 40 multiple-choice questions
- 60 minutes (extra time may be allowed for non-native English speakers if no translated paper is available)
- Pass mark of 26/40 or 65%
- No negative marking
- Closed book

This chapter contains guidance for those using this book to prepare for the ITIL Foundation exam.

Once you have passed your exam, you can use this book as a reference guide. You may not need to look at this chapter again.

The ITIL Foundation certificate

The Foundation certificate provides formal certification that a candidate has a good general understanding of ITIL concepts and practices. It is a compulsory, entry-level certificate that must be passed before candidates can take any higher-level ITIL certifications. This book provides you with all the information you need to pass the ITIL Foundation exam, as well as lots of extra information not covered in the syllabus.

If you're preparing for the exam, you should download a copy of the latest syllabus from the AXELOS website. You can use it to help direct your studies.

Sample exams

As part of your preparation, you should do as many sample exam questions as possible. You can download a free sample exam paper from the AXELOS website. Other questions are available on the Internet, but remember that these may not be official, current or quality controlled.

Sample exams help you:

- Understand the question format and the language used
- Test your time management strategies
- Gauge your readiness for the real thing

We're going to discuss some strategies for multiple-choice exams.

The ITIL Foundation exam has 40 questions and lasts for one hour. You need to get 26 correct to pass – the pass percentage is 65%. The exam is closed book, and there are no trick questions or negative marking.

Approaching multiple-choice exams

Here are some general points to remember when you sit any exam:

- **Read the question carefully:** if you're not careful, you will answer the question you think you see, not the one that's actually on the paper. We're all trained to speed read these days – try dragging your finger along the question so you don't miss a vital word (like 'NOT').
- **Don't panic!:** if your mind goes blank, move on and look at something else. Your subconscious mind will work away even when you're answering a different question.

- **Use the process of elimination:** each question has four possible answers – if you can discount one or two, you've dramatically increased your odds of picking the right answer.
- **Trust your instinct:** one of the most common pieces of exam feedback I've heard is from candidates who wish they hadn't changed their answer. It's fine to check over what you've done but be very wary about changing your mind.
- **Manage your time:** you have one-and-a-half minutes per question. I've never yet met a candidate who told me they ran out of time on the Foundation exam, but some have come close! Don't spend too long staring at one question, when there are easy marks to be picked up further on in the paper.
- **Use the 'four sweep' approach:** on your first sweep through the exam paper, pick off the easy questions. If you've answered 23 questions easily, that takes the pressure off for your second sweep. Sweep two: spend more time on the challenging questions but leave anything you really don't know for sweep three. Calculate how many answers you're confident of again. Sweep three: pick off those tough questions. Finally, sweep four: the sense check. Be wary of changing your answers, but look out for that question where you knew the answer was D and you've written C by mistake.

I hope you've enjoyed this book, and I wish you every success with your ITIL Foundation exam and your ITSM career.

BIBLIOGRAPHY

- *Accelerate: Building Strategic Agility for a Faster-Moving World*, 2014, J.P. Kotter, Harvard Business Review Press.
- Blue ocean/red ocean source: Kim, WC & Mauborgne, R 2015, *Blue ocean strategy*, exp. edn. p. 140. HBS Publishing, Boston.
- *Game On! Change is Constant: Tactics to Win When Leading Change is Everyone's Business*, 2019, Karen Ferris, BookPOD.
- *ITIL® Foundation, ITIL 4 Edition*, 2019, AXELOS Limited.
- "Observability". Honeycomb.io *www.honeycomb.io/observability/*.
- *SIAM Foundation Body of Knowledge*, C. Agutter ao.
- *SIAM Professional Body of Knowledge*, M. Major-Goldsmith, S. Dorst ao.
  Both available as free downloads at *www.scopism.com/free-downloads/*.
- "Swarming". J Hall, Medium.com *https://medium.com/@JonHall_/itsm-devops-and-why-the-three-tier-structure-must-be-replaced-with-swarming-91e76ba22304*.
- *The Site Reliability Workbook*, 2018, B. Beyer et al., O'Reilly Media, Inc.
- *VeriSM™: Unwrapped and Applied*, 2018, C. Agutter, J. Botha and S. D. Van Hove, Van Haren Publishing.

FURTHER READING

IT Governance Publishing (ITGP) is the world's leading publisher for governance and compliance. Our industry-leading pocket guides, books, training resources and toolkits are written by real-world practitioners and thought leaders. They are used globally by audiences of all levels, from students to C-suite executives.

Our high-quality publications cover all IT governance, risk and compliance frameworks and are available in a range of formats. This ensures our customers can access the information they need in the way they need it.

Our other publications about ITIL and ITSM include:

- *ITIL® Foundation Essentials ITIL 4 Edition – The ultimate revision guide, Second edition* by Claire Agutter,
  www.itgovernancepublishing.co.uk/product/itil-foundation-essentials-itil-4-edition
- *Pragmatic Application of Service Management – The Five Anchor Approach* by S. D. Van Hove and Mark Thomas,
  www.itgovernancepublishing.co.uk/product/pragmatic-application-of-service-management
- *Catalogs, Services and Portfolios – An ITSM success story* by Daniel McLean,
  www.itgovernancepublishing.co.uk/product/catalogs-services-and-portfolios

For more information on ITGP and branded publishing services, and to view our full list of publications, visit *www.itgovernancepublishing.co.uk*.

To receive regular updates from ITGP, including information on new publications in your area(s) of interest, sign up for our newsletter at
www.itgovernancepublishing.co.uk/topic/newsletter.

Branded publishing

Through our branded publishing service, you can customise ITGP publications with your company's branding.
Find out more at
www.itgovernancepublishing.co.uk/topic/branded-publishing-services.

Related services

ITGP is part of GRC International Group, which offers a comprehensive range of complementary products and services to help organisations meet their objectives.

For a full range of resources on ITIL visit *www.itgovernance.co.uk/shop/category/itil*.

Training services

The IT Governance training programme is built on our extensive practical experience designing and implementing management systems based on ISO standards, best practice and regulations.

Our courses help attendees develop practical skills and comply with contractual and regulatory requirements. They also support career development via recognised qualifications.

Learn more about our training courses in ITIL and view the full course catalogue at *www.itgovernance.co.uk/training*.

Professional services and consultancy

We are a leading global consultancy of IT governance, risk management and compliance solutions. We advise businesses around the world on their most critical issues and present cost-saving and risk-reducing solutions based on international best practice and frameworks.

We offer a wide range of delivery methods to suit all budgets, timescales and preferred project approaches.

Find out how our consultancy services can help your organisation at *www.itgovernance.co.uk/consulting*.

Industry news

Want to stay up to date with the latest developments and resources in the IT governance and compliance market? Subscribe to our Weekly Round-up newsletter and we will send you mobile-friendly emails with fresh news and features about your preferred areas of interest, as well as unmissable offers and free resources to help you successfully start your projects. *www.itgovernance.co.uk/weekly-round-up*.

EU for product safety is Stephen Evans, The Mill Enterprise Hub, Stagreenan, Drogheda, Co. Louth, A92 CD3D, Ireland. (servicecentre@itgovernance.eu)